Living In The Light

22 Creative Components Including Services, Dialogues, Monologues, Skits, Dramas, Meditations, And A Litany

Joe Barone

Joseph M. Beer

William R. Grimbol

Mary Hoover

Amy Jo Jones

Jeff Milsten

Diana M. Morris

CSS Publishing Company, Inc., Lima, Ohio

LIVING IN THE LIGHT

Copyright © 2008 by
CSS Publishing Company, Inc.
Lima, Ohio

The original purchaser may photocopy material in this publication for use as it was intended (worship material for worship use; educational material for classroom use; dramatic material for staging or production). No additional permission is required from the publisher for such copying by the original purchaser only. Inquiries should be addressed to: Permissions, CSS Publishing Company, Inc., 517 South Main Street, Lima, Ohio 45804.

Some scripture quotations are from the New Revised Standard Version of the Bible, copyright 1989 by the Division of Christian Education of the National Council of Churches of Christ in the USA. Used by permission.

Some scripture quotations are from the Revised Standard Version of the Bible, copyrighted 1946, 1952 ©, 1971, 1973, by the Division of Christian Education of the National Council of the Churches of Christ in the USA. Used by permission.

The section written by William R. Grimbol was taken from *Passion Paths*, published by CSS Publishing Company, Inc., in 1987, ISBN: 0-89536-842-0.

The section written by Joe Barone was taken from *My Tomb Was Empty*, published by CSS Publishing Company, Inc., in 1993, ISBN: 1-55673-564-2.

For more information about CSS Publishing Company resources, visit our website at www.csspub.com or email us at custserv@csspub.com or call (800) 241-4056.

Cover design by Barbara Spencer
ISBN-13: 978-0-7880-2502-0
ISBN-10: 0-7880-2502-3

PRINTED IN USA

Table Of Contents

Ash Wednesday
   The Path Of Maturity — 7
   An Introduction, Worship Service, and Dramatic Reading
   by William R. Grimbol

Lent 1
   Two Blind Men — 17
   A Dialogue by Diana M. Morris

Lent 2
   Moneybag — 21
   A Monologue by Diana M. Morris

   Simon, Brother Of Jesus — 23
   A Midweek Monologue by Diana M. Morris

Lent 3
   Crippled Woman — 27
   A Monologue by Diana M. Morris

   Centurion Darius And His Sister, Cassia — 29
   A Midweek Skit by Diana M. Morris

Lent 4
   Zacchaeus — 35
   A Skit by Diana M. Morris

   Nicodemus And Joseph Of Arimathea — 39
   A Midweek Dialogue by Diana M. Morris

Lent 5
   Innocent Of The Blood Of Jesus — 45
   A Monologue by Joe Barone

   Alexander And Rufus: Sons Of Simon Of Cyrene — 47
   A Midweek Skit by Diana M. Morris

Passion/Palm Sunday
   Hosanna! Save Now!* — 53
   An Introduction and Monologue by Amy Jo Jones

Maundy Thursday
    The Eyes Of Jesus   61
    An Introduction, Worship Service, and Monologue
    by Amy Jo Jones

    We Worship You   69
    A Litany by Jeff Milsten

Good Friday
    See How He Died*   73
    A Monologue by Amy Jo Jones

    All Are Worthy   77
    A Play by Joseph M. Beer

Easter Vigil
    Introduction   107

    Day Of Nothing — So Why Are We Here?   109
    A Worship Service with a choice of two Meditations
    by Mary Hoover and Amy Jo Jones

    Will You Live In The Light?   121
    A Worship Service and Meditation
    by Mary Hoover and Amy Jo Jones

    The Living Will And Testament Of Jesus Christ   125
    A Worship Service and Meditation
    by Mary Hoover and Amy Jo Jones

Easter Day
    Do You Believe?*   131
    A Monologue by Amy Jo Jones

    Mary Clopas   135
    A Monologue by Diana M. Morris

About The Authors   137

*This is a three-part monologue series using the same character.

Ash Wednesday

The Path Of Maturity

*An Introduction, Worship Service, and Dramatic Reading
by William R. Grimbol*

Ash Wednesday
Introduction

The Path Of Maturity

Lent is a time when we must dig down deep inside ourselves in order to explore the scope of our sin, as well as the decay of our low level of discipleship. Such a rigorous venture will often leave us anxious and guilt-ridden and certain that we will never find our way out of this maze of mistakes. The passion path illuminated in the worship service and dramatic reading is a very real attempt to help us make what Edna Hong chose to call, in her book of the same title, a "downward ascent."

The responsive reading in the worship service can use a lay leader rather than a pastor, and one should feel free to use lay participants for any part of the service where it is believed to be appropriate. The service was written with the intention of being as flexible as possible in this regard.

The dramatic reading should be done without costuming, any significant staging, or any other typical theater trappings. The goal is to be stark and simple, and to retain a sermonic look and feel. I should suggest simply the use of a spotlight, or some other very basic device to call attention to the various readers.

Ash Wednesday
Worship Service

The Path Of Maturity

Prelude

Call To Worship
Pastor: We come to this service to get in tune and in touch, with our hearts, our spirits, and our souls.
People: Free us, O God, to go down deep inside ourselves, and to penetrate the core of love at our center.
Pastor: Enable us, O God, to make the downward ascent during this mysterious and miraculous Lenten season.
People: Lent is a painful time of fearless examination, and yet, also a time of significant renewal.
All: We come ready for both the scrutiny and the restoration, ready to go down inside ourselves, as well as up into the eternal embrace of your love. Amen.

Hymn
"Beneath The Cross Of Jesus"

Silent Confession

Words Of Absolution
Pastor: Whenever we feel that our lives are as barren and brittle as a naked tree in the midst of winter, remind us, Lord, that beneath the surface of our souls, your molten grace is preparing the blossoms and buds of a forever spring. Remind us, Lord, that your forgiveness heals and renews us, even when we cannot sense your presence.
People: We give thanks for the gift of your life, a gift that comforts and consoles, a gift that cauterizes and confronts, and a gift that resurrects our energy and excitement for life. Amen.

Scripture Reading Psalm 90

Anthem/Solo

Scripture Reading Ephesians 4:1-16

Hymn "In The Cross Of Christ I Glory"

Sermon Dramatic Reading: "The Path Of Maturity"

Quiet Meditation

Offering

Offertory

Litany

Pastor: We have myriad excuses for our failure to love, O Christ, and even we are weary of them.

People: Grant us the courage and the conviction to never stop working on our loving, to never stop listening, to never stop caring, to never stop forgiving, to never stop embracing, to never stop granting to others our understanding — our respect — our compassion, and to never stop believing in the power of love to bind the brokenhearted, to heal and make whole, and to create an abundant hope.

All: **To love is our greatest calling. To love is our greatest challenge. To love is our greatest triumph. To love is our greatest testimony of faith. Amen.**

Sacrament Of The Lord's Supper

Words Of Preparation

Pastor: As we celebrate communion, let us be scorched with the awareness that to lead a life of mature loving will, as it did for Christ, requires all that we are. Let us be scalded with the consciousness that mature loving always leads to a cross.

Words Of Institution

"Come to me, all who labor and are heavy laden, and I will give you rest" (Matthew 11:28 RSV).

That invitation still stands for the followers of Jesus. He is here, he is the host for this meal. He is the one who promises us forgiveness. He is the one who assures us of eternal life. We are his disciples, and as we gather around this table, our faith in him binds us together as brothers and sisters.

Hear the words from the upper room: "In the night in which he was betrayed, our Lord Jesus took bread, and gave thanks; broke it, and gave it to his disciples, saying, 'Take and eat; this is my body, given for you. Do this for the remembrance of me.'"

Communion

The Lord's Prayer

Passing Of The Peace

Unison Reading 1 Corinthians 12:31—13:13 (RSV)

Earnestly desire the higher gifts.
And I will show you a still more excellent way.
If I speak in the tongues of men and of angels, but have not love, I am a noisy gong or a clanging cymbal. And if I have prophetic powers, and understand all mysteries and all knowledge, and if I have all faith, so as to remove mountains, but have not love, I am nothing. If I give away all I have, and if I deliver my body to be burned, but have not love, I gain nothing.

Love is patient and kind; love is not jealous or boastful; it is not arrogant or rude. Love does not insist on its own way; it is not irritable or resentful; it does not rejoice at wrong, but rejoices in the right. Love bears all things, believes all things, hopes all things, endures all things.

Love never ends, as for prophecy, it will pass away; as for tongues, they will cease; as for knowledge, it will pass away. For our knowledge is imperfect and our prophecy is imperfect; but when the perfect comes, the imperfect will pass away. When I was a child, I spoke like a child, I thought like a

child, I reasoned like a child; when I became a man, I gave up childish ways. For now we see in a mirror dimly, but then face to face. Now I know in part; then I shall understand fully, even as I have been fully understood. So faith, hope, love abide, these three; but the greatest of these is love.

Hymn "When I Survey The Wondrous Cross"

Benediction
Pastor: Let us depart in peace, emboldened by the cross to be reckless and rigorous in our loving. And let our loving always reflect the maturity that the cross demands of all disciples. Amen.

Postlude

Ash Wednesday
Dramatic Reading

The Path Of Maturity

Note: This dramatic reading requires five readers.

Reader 1: Somehow, Lord, everywhere we look in scripture, the concept of maturity is always fused with our capacity to love, and our capacity to love is always bonded to our ability to first love ourselves. Why? Why did you have to make the task of maturation so brutally simple ... so crucifyingly modest? Why does our maturation migration always have to wing its way home to the context of loving ... the art of loving ... the work of loving? It is just such a naive notion, such an idealistic and sentimental vision, and such an exercise in hopeless frustration. If our maturity is always to be measured by the extent and depth of our commitment to loving, then we are all hopelessly destined to lives of foolishness and childishness. Even at the beginning we are utter failures; to love ourselves seems impossible!

Lord, we have so much to dislike in ourselves, so much we find pathetic and phony and false. We are possessed by possessions. We are addicted to accumulation. We hide behind ridiculous images — masks — titles — brands. We have grown callous to what we feel. We have grown bored with what we think. We have grown indifferent to what we think. We have grown indifferent to what we believe. We seldom ever dream, set new goals, make new friends, or even seem able to embrace and enjoy life. For most of us, life is just an endurance test that nobody passes, and the most we can hope for is to endure — to kill some time, waste some time, or spend some time. Who could ever have imagined that *time* would become our most feared enemy?

We are ashamed, Lord, of our laziness, our lack of courage, our lack of hope, and our lack of faith. We are embarrassed with how little time we actually devote to the art of loving and how seldom we strive to fulfill your call to love with reckless abandon. But Lord, we just don't love ourselves, we just don't believe that our lives are really worth that much. We just don't believe that life has all that much to offer, except the good life, and that is so bankrupt ethically, because it has nothing whatsoever to do with goodness. We must start with ourselves, but there just seems to be so little there worth loving ... so little there for which we feel genuine pride ... so little there for which we feel genuine pride ... so little there for which we feel you might be proud. Maturity? Loving? We fall so miserably short.

Reader 2: Next, you ask us to love our neighbor as ourself. Our neighbor — who is that? There once was a time when we sat on front porches, and chatted with our neighbors, but these days we hide behind backyard fences, and screened-in patios. We fear our neighbors. They are our competition. They are our opponents in the mad scramble up the ladder of success. Our neighbors might find out our flaws or our failings, they might uncover our fragility and vulnerability, or they might expose the frightening child that lurks within that tough and together exterior. Our neighbors are not to be trusted. They might steal our piece of the pie. They might get a higher rank on the success ladder. They might wear more designer labels. Loving our neighbors, Lord, once again you prove how out of touch and unaware you are of reality — the real world.

Reader 3: When it comes to loving the world, you just expect too much — way, way too much. You were such an idealist; I mean, you loved anybody and everybody, regardless of status or position, regardless of role or rank, regardless of color or religion, and regardless of sin or crime. As sensible religious folks, we claim to love these outcasts, but we are smart enough to not go near them, so we don't get smudged or stained by their "loser" qualities, or by their flagrant flaws, or their massive mistakes. You went right into their midst, right into the middle of that moral squalor, and you kept on celebrating the miracles you insisted that you found in all of that bland, boring, mundane existence. Such an idealist!

Reader 4: You even had the gall to ask us to love our enemies. What mature person really loves their enemies? Not any mature person I know. Were you a pacifist? Honestly, I mean if you really meant it, to love our enemies, then the bottom line is that you had to be a pacifist. Loving our enemies means giving up our weapons — our weaponry of grudges and resentments, our weaponry of past injustices and humiliations, our weaponry of known defects and inadequacies in others, our weaponry of righteous indignation and smug morality, our weaponry of superior intellect and aristocratic arrogance, and our weaponry of warmaking like the bombs and bullets that now threaten to blast creation back to chaos again. Do you really expect us to give up our weapons? Do you really expect us to be peacemakers? Do you really expect us to love our enemies? That means knowing them, understanding them, accepting them, living side by side with them, respecting them, and forgiving them. Do you really mean loving them?

Reader 5: Christ did mean it. He meant exactly what he said, and that call to radical, reckless, rigorous loving remains to this day the most troublesome message of his ministry. Christ has called us all to pass the acid test of faith, which is to always keep on widening the scope of our loving, and to know that our loving is also that which serves as a sacred symbol of our maturity, as a sign of our growing up into Christ, who is the author of all loving.

Christ did mean it, but he also meant that if we will only work on our loving relationship with him, the love will burst forth out of us like lava from a volcano. If we will only work, and I mean work hard, at our intimacy with Christ, our prayer life, our study of scripture, our peacemaking, our pursuit of justice, our service and our sacrifice, our forgiving and being forgiven, and our tender mercies, administered to a tortured and troubled world, then, and only then, we can fulfill the mature call to obedient loving. Then, and only then, can we find within ourselves the courage necessary to pick up our crosses and follow him who is our Lord and Savior.

He meant it!

He meant every word!

There is simply no denying the truth that maturity and loving are like spiritual Siamese twins, and that discipleship is the life lived by those who know the spiritual seal of those fused and bonded concepts and actions.

Maturity and loving, they are one and the same, and one without the other is like a cross without a resurrection, or an Easter without a Good Friday.

Lent 1

Two Blind Men

***A Dialogue*
by Diana M. Morris**

Lent 1
Dialogue

Two Blind Men
Deuteronomy 26:1-11

Characters
   Aaron — middle-aged man
   Jacob — middle-aged man

Props
   None required

Setting
   None required

Costumes
   Use period costumes — robes, sandals, head coverings, and the like

(Jacob comes in from the aisle and Aaron comes from the side aisle to meet at the chancel area. They have not seen each other for a long time. They embrace.)

Aaron: *(ironically)* My old friend, it's so good to *see* you.

Jacob: *(chuckles, then says ironically)* And for me to *see* you, Aaron. What is it now, five years?

Aaron: Yes, and four of those since Jesus' resurrection. It doesn't seem possible. How are you?

Jacob: I'm better now than I was. After I regained my sight, I couldn't figure out what I could do for a living. What was I to do? How *was* I to live and where? After all, I was born blind and never learned a trade. I only learned how to beg at the gate.

Aaron: I understand. At least I had learned carpentry before I lost my sight. But what did you do?

Jacob: A new friend, one who was following Jesus, helped me learn to be a shepherd. Shepherds are treated as badly as those of us who have to beg for a living. But, being a shepherd taught me more about Jesus' teachings and more about his parables. After a while I started following some of Jesus' disciples instead of tending sheep. I still find it amazing that our Lord rose from the dead! But I know it's true.

Aaron: I've been with Paul and a few others when they went to Corinth and then back to Jerusalem. I must ask you, though, are you still amazed at so much beauty to see? The beauty of the stars at night, water droplets that magnify rainbows, flowers and cypress trees, sunrises and sunsets — all of it is overwhelming at times.

Jacob: What amazes me all the time is the beauty in peoples' faces, each of them with such different personalities, and all the different animals. Then there is the sweetness of small children, especially when they are sleeping — or even if the child is wide awake and crying!

Aaron: That's all true. I still remember the very first thing I saw. I saw the face of Jesus. Do you remember that?

Jacob: I could never forget. His face just reflected love and compassion. Yet, the decision of our healing was up to us, he said, and our faith and belief that Jesus was the Son of God. How could we have known when we called out to him to heal us that it wasn't just our sight he would heal?

Aaron: I've often wondered what would have happened if we had listened to the crowd yelling at us to be quiet? If we had not called out, where would we be now? We had heard of Jesus and that he was coming our way.

Jacob: Yes, and when we heard about him, we believed right away that he was the chosen one, the Messiah.

Aaron: But we couldn't keep quiet and even the crowd saw our healing. We had to go and tell everyone that the Messiah healed us — that we could see!

Jacob: I wish some of the things we didn't have to see, like those who didn't have the chance to see Jesus as we did and those who are empty inside, who have no life within them. But the worst sight was seeing Jesus crucified. Do you remember how dark it became as he died? For a moment I thought I was losing my sight again because it was only three o'clock in the afternoon.

Aaron: I, too, thought I was losing my sight again as I stood there and watched him take his last breath. But later, the next week, I heard that Jesus had risen from the grave and once again, immediately actually, I believed it. He was, and is, my Lord. I'll travel with his other followers to tell everyone all he taught us and who he is.

Jacob: I must go. I'm meeting with some of his followers yet this afternoon and as you know, we have to be careful where we meet and who we tell about him. But I, too, can hardly contain myself about my Lord and Savior, Jesus Christ. Shalom, my friend, and may we meet again soon.

Aaron: Shalom, Jacob. God go with you!

(They leave the opposite way from where they came in.)

Lent 2

Moneybag

A Monologue
by Diana M. Morris

Simon, Brother Of Jesus

A Midweek Monologue
by Diana M. Morris

Lent 2
Monologue

Moneybag
Luke 13:31-35

Character
　Moneybag (offstage voice)

Props
　Table
　Moneybag
　Coins
　Microphone

Setting
　Stage with spotlight

Costume
　None required

(A moneybag is sitting on a table in the center of the chancel area with coins on it, around it, and down on the floor. A spotlight is on the moneybag and the person doing the monologue is out of sight with a microphone.)

Moneybag: You might wonder what a moneybag is doing talking to you in this season of Lent, a time when we think about Jesus and his trip to Jerusalem. Well, Jesus and money were always intertwined, from his birth and the rich gifts he was given, to his betrayal by Judas. And Judas — taking the thirty silver coins given to him by the Sanhedrin — asked these men to take back the money. But they would not take it back. "I have sinned," he said, and, "I have betrayed innocent blood." It was at this time that Judas threw the coins on the floor and back to the Pharisees.

　What do we know about the money of Jesus' day? We know that there were two kinds of coins. The first were the Roman coins marked with an image of Caesar and the second were the temple coins used by the moneychangers in the outer part of the temple. That was where Roman money was exchanged for Jewish coins. There is something about me that was true in Jesus' time and is still true in the present time. There is never enough of me. If you are poor and can hardly pay the bills, you want more money. Likewise, when you have a lot of money, you still want more of it. There is never enough of me. People always want more and more.

　Did you know that Jesus actually talked about money more than anything else? The money issue was in his parables, in his teachings, and in his life from the beginning until he took a whip and chased all of those moneylenders out of the temple at Jerusalem.

　Jesus saw to it that Judas handled the money for Jesus and his followers, as a group. Isn't it interesting that we never hear of Judas being qualified to handle money? And yet, we hear about Matthew being a former tax collector. Obviously, he was qualified to handle money even when he cheated lots of people as a tax collector.

All of the disciples, not just Judas, complained about the extravagance of the ointment that the woman used to anoint Jesus' feet and head. It wasn't just Judas who complained. These disciples believed that this could have been sold and the proceeds given to the poor. It was worth a year's wages. Judas did not say this because he cared about the poor, but because he was a thief; as keeper of the moneybag, he used to help himself to what was put in.

Jesus, himself, had no money. When he was crucified, he had no money, just his cloak, and the guards rolled dice to see who would win it.

I remember well the parable about the man who issued coins to his three workers, giving the first man ten coins, the second man five coins, and the third man one coin. These men were to invest these coins and make more money for the master. The first two men did make more money for their employer, but the third man was afraid of losing his one coin and therefore, he buried it. The two men who made money were told that they were good and faithful servants. The third man was called a lazy and wicked servant and even his one coin was taken away from him.

I have often wondered what the man who owned the pigs felt about Jesus. You remember that story, the herd of pigs was invaded by evil spirits, so Jesus told the spirits to leave and then the herd of pigs ran off the cliff and was killed. Did Jesus think about the cost of all these pigs and what it would do to their owner? We don't know from the story, but I bet Jesus did know the cost.

One day, Jesus gave the people the blessings you call the Beatitudes. He told the disciples that the people, about 5,000 of them, plus women and children, were hungry and needed fed. He asked the disciples to feed the 5,000, but the disciples did not know how they could do this. Judas told them that they didn't have that much money, and the others agreed. They told Jesus to send the people away. Jesus was then given two little fish and five loaves of bread. He blessed them and then asked the disciples to give that meager amount of food to the crowd. They did, and they had twelve baskets left over. Remember, when you share of me there is always more than enough.

Many cruel things have been done to people because of me — because of money! There have been wars, robberies, greed, and deaths. The crusades were some of the worst of the wars and deaths because of me. Some of the thousands who were killed in just the last century, and even the current wars, are all for money in one way or another. However, most of these things are because of the *love* of money. Money, itself, isn't bad or sinful; money can do so much good.

Do you want to be me or another bag of money in either coins or paper bills? Do you want to be rich and have enough? What would you do to have a moneybag of your own? Think before you answer, for each decision you make about money is a time of crossroads, a time of decision.

Think before you answer!

(Spotlight turns off immediately after the last word is spoken.)

Lent 2
Midweek Monologue

Simon, Brother Of Jesus
Matthew 13:10-17

Character
Simon — young adult male

Props
None required

Setting
None required

Costume
Simon is dressed shepherd-like — sandals, head covering, and so on

Simon: You've heard many things about two of my brothers. There were five brothers in my family and several sisters, and you've probably never even heard their names. The women of my time were considered of no use, even though they kept the house, taught the early lessons to the children, sewed clothes, and so on.

One of my brothers changed the world, not just in my time, but forever, and in every land. My next oldest brother followed in the first one's footsteps, at least as well as he was able. The five brothers were James, Joseph, Judas, Jesus, and me. My name is Simon. Jesus was the firstborn and I was the last of all the brothers and sisters. I'm the baby of the family. I was very young, a teenager you would call me now, when Jesus was baptized. It was at that time that he was gone in the wilderness for a long time. Some of the family thought he was dead. However, when he came back from the wilderness, he was changed.

Almost from the very beginning, the Jewish authorities were upset with my big brother. I couldn't understand this because I had always looked up to Jesus. He was an accomplished carpenter, too. He was so loving and caring about each of us. Our village of Nazareth loved him. However, with our father, Joseph, dead, the villagers couldn't understand why Jesus would go away, why he was not married, and why he didn't stay to help his mother to whom he had always been the closest. It wasn't until after Jesus was crucified and then arose from the grave that James became the leader of the church in Jerusalem. So, you see, the two oldest brothers didn't live as was expected of them. Our family was full of different crossroads. We children heard people talk about mother being with child before she and my father were married.

Then again, it was interesting, too, that as the church grew, so did the stories about Jesus. People would ask our mother, Mary, about Jesus. Was he born at home, was he sick as a baby, and is that why Mary, Joseph, and Jesus went to Egypt for several years? So the stories began and were added to, at times. I always thought there was something special about my big brother, but in a kind way. I heard that the family went to hear Jesus, and then wanted to take him home because they thought he was crazy. Jesus rebuked them all. Our family was outraged that he would treat our mother that way. However, although she was hurt, she understood and they went back to Nazareth. It was later that our mother started following Jesus and listening to her oldest son. She remained faithful as she saw him beaten, crucified, and buried. She even held her dead son in her arms before they took him to a tomb owned by a very rich man, named Joseph of Arimathea, a member of the Sanhedrin. She was also there to see the empty tomb and then to see Jesus in the upper room. No one but the family knows that he came to say good-bye to all of us, too. By that time we knew that yes, he was human, and yes, he was the Son of God.

Lent 3

Crippled Woman

A Monologue
by Diana M. Morris

Centurion Darius And His Sister, Cassia

A Midweek Skit
by Diana M. Morris

Lent 3
Monologue

Crippled Woman
Luke 13:10-17

Character
  Rachel — middle-aged woman

Props
  None required

Setting
  None required

Costume
  Rachel is dressed in period clothing

Rachel: Hello, my name is Rachel and my story brings a lot of people to a crossroads in their lives. You see, several things happened over eighteen years. You'll hear me talking about my childhood friend, Adah. You'll hear about several people in my story.

Let's start eighteen years and one month ago. Adah told me that she saw the very beginning of my illness. I was having a hard time standing up straight and to do so was extremely painful, so I would bend over just a little bit to relieve the pain. Over the weeks and months and years, I ended up doubled over. The children made fun of me and I felt hopeless, defeated, like a failure, and very depressed. I had been to many physicians and healers over the years. I had to have help with everything: dressing, cleaning myself, cooking, even eating, and all of the things that we take for granted in our normal day. I did not marry because no one would have me and therefore I had no children because it would have been physically impossible. Most of the people in my village felt that I had a physical demon and that it was contagious, which wasn't true.

My story is intertwined with Jesus of Nazareth, but those who wrote about him did not think that my story was important enough to tell what the name of my village was, or even that I had a name. I've taken a name just so I can tell you my story. I was not contagious, which they found out after weeks and months. Therefore, I was not shunned like those with leprosy were. In your time, there is a name for my disease. It is called Ankylosing Spondylitis (ankle-lo-sing spon-dil-i-tis) and even though 2,000 years have past since Jesus was on earth, there is still no cure for this painful disease. The disease is a form of progressive arthritis with inflammation and stiffness. Eventually, the spinal bones fuse together, which makes my story even more of a miracle! All that can be done for the people with this disease is to try to manage their pain. My spine had fused entirely and I was bent over double, which is very bad for the rest of your body and its organs. Literally, I was bound by my body, virtually bound with invisible chains of calcium that had hardened my spine.

I'm not sure why I went to the synagogue that sabbath day. I did not go often because of the jeering from the children and just because it was so painful to get there. I was in the back of the congregation, in back of all the women, actually, but I couldn't be invisible appearing the way I did. To act like I wasn't there was impossible. I had heard about this Jesus. Reports of his teachings were rampant throughout the village, but I didn't go to the synagogue for him to heal me because I'd given up after so many doctors and healers were unable to do anything for me.

Jesus had just finished one of his teaching stories, the last one according to Luke's writings, then he got up and called my name to come to him. Most people who were healed went searching for Jesus. I did not. Everyone was watching and wondering what I'd done to get this specific attention. I really couldn't see Jesus well because I was bent double. My depression about my illness and my pain was a great deal like a physical demon. There was a hush over all the crowd as I inched my way forward and my friend, Adah, touched my hand as I moved forward, giving me comfort. I will never forget that moment. Jesus said to me, "Woman, you are set free from your infirmity" and then he laid his hands on my back and *immediately*, with no hesitation, I stood up straight. I could take the first good breath that I'd had in years and years. Then I began to praise God! I gave my all in praise of God and of my healing through Jesus. The crowd was grinning from ear to ear, my friends were praising God, and some were laughing. My friend, Adah, was crying and laughing at the same time.

Then the funniest thing happened, at least I thought it was funny. I saw that the leader of the synagogue was angry and the more he acted out his anger, the more I praised God. But Jesus was angry with this man and told him that he was a hypocrite! This leader said it was unlawful to heal on the sabbath according to the Fourth Commandment. Jesus said to him and his followers, "Does not each one of you on the sabbath untie his ox or his donkey from the manger and lead it out for watering? This daughter of Abraham, who has been bound for eighteen years now, ought she not to have been set free on the sabbath day from this bondage?" Indeed, when Jesus had said these things, his adversaries were humiliated and the whole crowd rejoiced at all the splendid deeds done by Jesus.

Then, Adah and I were walking and dancing together, for I was healed! I was healed by the power of God through Jesus. Now you know the rest of my story!

It troubles me, though, because I've heard some rumors that the authorities are trying to snare Jesus. I understand he's going to Jerusalem soon. I pray for Jesus constantly. Maybe you should, too.

Lent 3
Midweek Skit

Centurion Darius And His Sister, Cassia
Matthew 8:5-14, 27-54; Mark 15:39

Characters
    Darius
    Cassia

Props
    Table and chair
    Papers and pen

Setting
    None required, but a spotlight could focus on the speaking character as the scene switches back and forth

Costumes
    Use costumes from the period

(Darius is seated at a table, writing a letter, and speaking as he writes.)

Darius: Dear Cassia,
    I hope this finds you well. Thank you for your last letter telling me how our parents are. You are such a good listener through these letters. I can tell because you seem to write back to me as soon as you receive a letter.
    I have been very troubled of late. I told you several letters ago of how ill my manservant, Faustus, has been. Well, now I must tell you about his healing and tell you the end of the story.
    Several weeks ago, one of my soldiers informed me that there was an itinerant Hebrew preacher who was also noted for his ability to heal. They told me his name was Jesus and that his hometown was Nazareth. It's just a very little village and not noted for anything in particular. They said he was very close right now, even though he has been wandering all over Galilee and was slowly heading south toward Jerusalem. I went looking for him and found him just as he was coming into Capernaum. I said to him, "Lord, my servant, Faustus, lies at home paralyzed and in terrible suffering." Jesus told me that he would come with me and heal him, but I told him that was not necessary, that I didn't deserve to have him come under my roof. I told him that I was a man under authority, with soldiers under me and that if I tell one to "go," he goes; or to "come," and he comes to my command. Jesus seemed astonished at my faith and said so to his followers. Then he told me to go back home and I would find my servant well. And when I got home, Faustus was healed! *(fades out as Cassia picks up)*

(Cassia quietly enters from the other side of the stage, reading Darius' letter. She picks up where he has faded out.)

Cassia: I knew that this man was a prophet of the Hebrew people. Once in a while, I heard about his healings, but he never seemed to make any problems for my soldiers and me. That changed one Sunday afternoon. A crowd of people started taking off their cloaks and laying them on the road into Jerusalem. They did this waving palm branches, you know, the big ones. Then I saw Jesus riding in on a donkey. To tell the truth my soldiers said he looked rather ridiculous as his legs were almost on the ground because the donkey was so short. They said the people were hailing him with the phrase, "Hosanna! Blessed is the King of Israel that comes in the name of the Lord." *(fades out as Darius picks up)*

Darius: There were not that many people and it really lasted a short time. It wasn't until the next day that things began to change. Jesus walked into the Jewish temple and started a ruckus with a whip. He began to chase out all the moneychangers and the sellers of animals for sacrifice. Nothing else happened, but because of the uproar, Pilate ordered more troops onto the streets to quell any more problems. All the soldiers were upset with more work, and it was beginning to feel like a tightrope. The Jews began to celebrate their holiday on Thursday night. Only thirty of my cohorts had to be near Pilate. That night, Jesus was arrested in a garden and taken to the Jewish authorities, called the Sanhedrin. They forced him to go to Pilate who could find no fault with him. But these particular authorities wanted Jesus crucified and on Friday morning they had encouraged many of the crowd to ask Pilate to crucify him. *(fades out as Cassia picks up)*

Cassia: I was told to take care of the crucifixion of Jesus and the two other men who were thieves. First, my men tied Jesus to a post and proceeded to whip him. He was so bloody and weak. They also made fun of him by making a crown of thorns and placing it on his head so that these large thorns were forced into his scalp and forehead. They gave him a robe and a palm branch and then they spat on him. When they took the robe off, his wounds started to bleed all over again. Then it was time to take him to that hill that was really the city dump. The people called it Golgotha or "the place of the skull." As we marched the three men up to that hill, they were also made to carry their crosspiece on their shoulders. Jesus stumbled twice and the second time I grabbed this strong-looking fellow to carry Jesus' cross. I noticed that he had two boys with him, but that didn't stop me. *(fades out as Darius picks up)*

Darius: It took several groups of my men to get the three men nailed to their crosses. It seemed that Jesus was hallucinating, because he kept talking to his "father" and there was no male there that would have been his father. As a matter of fact, there was one man about Jesus' age with a group of about three or four women right at the foot of the cross. Someone told me that one of the women was his mother. I don't understand how she could have stood there to watch this cruel and horrible form of dying. I kept listening to his words, and I kept thinking about my servant, Faustus, that Jesus had healed. Why was this good man being put to death? I would have given anything to not be there. However, that was what I was ordered to do and there was no way I could change that. At close to three o'clock in the afternoon, Jesus said, "It is finished," and appeared to have died. I took my sword and put it in his side and blood came out, but there was no movement of his body. *(fades out as Cassia picks up)*

Cassia: Do you remember when I was hurt when we were children and the large scar that I had ever since then? Well, when Jesus' blood sprayed on me, it touched that scar and then healed it! *(acts surprised)* I just couldn't believe it even though I knew that he had healed Faustus from afar. Anyway, I remember saying, "Truly this man was the Son of God." I said it, but I wasn't sure what all that meant until later. But that wasn't the end of it. Two of the Jews from the Sanhedrin had gone to Pilate to ask for the body of Jesus and to bury him in a brand-new tomb belonging to one of them. I think his name was Joseph. *(fades out as Darius picks up)*

Darius: I thought this would be the end of these happenings. But other Jews were worried that Jesus' disciples would carry the body away because Jesus had said that he would rise again. I was called to see Pilate and he asked that I put a guard on the tomb for several days and nights. The first night was uneventful, but on Sunday morning at dawn, my guards felt a mighty earthquake and saw a bright light. The stone was rolled away of its own accord. My men were frightened and they hurried back to inform me and then I had to tell Pilate! It's too long a story to tell you what became of those few soldiers of mine. On the day Jesus died, because it was their sabbath, they did not have time to bury him with the burial spices, so on Sunday, at dawn, a small group of women came to where the tomb was. They went into the tomb, but Jesus wasn't there! I'm told that they hurried back to Jesus' disciples to tell them. Cassia, I must tell you this, but you must not tell a soul, because it could end my life and the lives of many others: I have become a follower of Jesus. I, too, believe that Jesus rose from the dead that morning and is alive, and some day those of us that believe — Jew and Gentile — will be with him in the next life. I want to get back to Rome to tell you all about this Jesus, this Son of God, the only God. *(fades out as Cassia picks up)*

Cassia: I want to tell you the whole story about Jesus and his teachings and his gift of new life with God. One more thing, the Jewish temple has a place that only the rabbi may go into and it is called the "holy of holies." There is a curtain between this place and the rest of the worship area. When Jesus died, at that very moment in the darkest skies you've ever seen at three o'clock in the afternoon, the curtain in the temple was torn in two. One of Jesus' disciples, named Peter, explained from that moment, no one had to come to God through an intercessor. Because Jesus died for each of us, now we can each come to God — this holy God, who gave his precious Son, on our own. *(fades out as Darius picks up)*

Darius: Be well, Cassia. My love to you, dear sister. If I do not see you in this lifetime, then I will see you in the next one!

Lent 4

Zacchaeus

A Skit
by Diana M. Morris

Nicodemus And Joseph Of Arimathea

A Midweek Dialogue
by Diana M. Morris

Lent 4
Skit

Zacchaeus
Luke 15:1-3, 11b-32; 19:1-10

Characters
Zacchaeus
Narrator
Grandchild 1
Grandchild 2
Grandchild 3

Props
Chair

Setting
None required

Costumes
Use costumes of the period

(Zacchaeus, a short man, stands in front of a chair. When Narrator begins to talk, Zacchaeus sits down on a chair.)

Zacchaeus: Hello! You will know me by the children's story that will be told to you. Just remember, there is more to me than being in a tree! Here is my story, told by my grandchildren.

Narrator: *(stands off to the side)* This is the story of Zacchaeus.

(Grandchildren are quietly standing in front of Zacchaeus.)

Grandchild 1: Zacchaeus was a little man who wanted to see Jesus. He wasn't tall. He was very small.

Grandchild 2: One day, Zacchaeus heard that Jesus was coming to Jericho.

Grandchild 3: He heard them say he was coming that day.

Narrator: Zacchaeus decided to go where Jesus would be. He decided to go to Jericho. As Zacchaeus came near the place where Jesus was walking, he saw crowds of people.

Grandchild 3: People were there from everywhere. Zacchaeus tried to push his way through the crowd. He tried to get through. It was too hard to do.

Grandchild 2: Zacchaeus was determined to find another way to see Jesus. He looked around. No way could be found. Finally, Zacchaeus climbed a sycamore tree along the path.

Grandchild 1: He climbed that tree, Lord Jesus to see.

Narrator: When Jesus came to the sycamore tree, he called to Zacchaeus.

Grandchild 3: Climb down from the tree. You are special to me.

Narrator: Jesus told Zacchaeus to hurry because he was going to his house.

Grandchild 2: Come, keep up the pace. Let's hurry to your place.

Narrator: Zacchaeus welcomed Jesus gladly. Follow me. My guest you'll be.

Grandchild 1: Zacchaeus felt nine feet tall that day. He was a little man, but he felt so grand.

Narrator: Zacchaeus told Jesus,

Grandchild 2: Lord, here and now, I give half of my possessions to the poor, and if I have cheated anybody, I will pay them back four times the amount. I'll give half to the poor. To the others, I'll pay more.

Grandchild 1: He has repented.

Grandchild 2: He has been saved.

Grandchild 3: Alleluia! Alleluia!

All Grandchildren: Amen! Amen![1]

Zacchaeus: Well, by now you know that I am Zacchaeus! And I'm known around Jericho and different parts of Palestine to have kept my promises. I gave away my fortune and yes, most of it had been made by cheating. But I often wonder what my life would have been like if I had not encountered Jesus that day.

Would I have cared later when I heard he was crucified? And later still when I heard he was raised from the dead? Would I have believed?

Well, I've talked with his disciples so often since that wonderful day. The twelve are no longer twelve, but hundreds of believers. All of them are hearing about Jesus, his life and his teachings from Jerusalem to Rome. Many of the followers have to meet in secret because the authorities are trying to get rid of them and their gospel teachings. But it can't be stopped! After all, Jesus is the Son of God! And that's what I tell anyone who will listen.

But, let me go back to my questions and my fortune. If I had continued as a tax collector for the Romans, I would have continued to cheat others and would have been such a hard, unforgiving man who would have treated his wife and family cruelly, including my wonderful grandchildren, as strangers. After my encounter with Jesus and his coming to my house, "a sinner's house," I now know my family and cherish each of them and the new friends I've made. I am no longer hated. I am no longer a stranger to those who loved me and who love me still.

Jesus was right when he said, "Today salvation has come to this house, because this man, too, is a son of Abraham. For the Son of Man came to seek and to save what was lost." The Son of God came to me, Zacchaeus, and I am no longer lost.

Thanks be to God!

---

1. Connie Walters, *Reader's Theater Bible-based Dramas New Testament* (Grand Rapids, Michigan: School Specialty Publishing, 1995), pp. 63-64.

Lent 4
Midweek Dialogue

Nicodemus And Joseph Of Arimathea
John 3:1-9; 7:19-39; 19:38-39

Characters
    Narrator
    Nicodemus
    Joseph

Props
    None required

Setting
    None required

Costumes
    Use costumes of the period

(Nicodemus and Joseph of Arimathea come to the area around the pulpit. When Narrator begins to speak, the two men freeze. When Narrator is finished, then the men are animated again and walk to the middle of the chancel area.)

Narrator: These two men, Joseph of Arimathea and Nicodemus, are walking through the garden away from the tomb. Sabbath has already begun; Joseph has just had a tomb built for himself in the stone of the garden. They have just finished preparing Jesus' body for death using the expensive ointments that Nicodemus brought.

Nicodemus: Joseph, I'm so grateful that your servants were able to help us with the stone, but I'm also pleased that you dismissed them before Shabbos began. It makes no difference about the two of us, as we are unclean anyhow with having touched Jesus' body. The seal mixture should keep that stone in place for eternity.

Joseph: The stone was far too heavy for the two of us and the soldiers wouldn't help anymore. It was luck that their centurion, I believe his name was Darius, ordered them to help us get Jesus down from the cross. Hopefully, my servants got back home in time for Shabbos. At least they didn't have to touch the body.

Nicodemus: I didn't think it would end this way.

Joseph: Nor did I. Oh, how I wish that I had come forward sooner, but I was too afraid of losing my position, my riches, my seat on the Sanhedrin, and my role as teacher. It's all gone now, but I was not going to let Jesus' body hang there for the birds and weather as the other Roman criminals. He was my Lord and I finally had to take a stand. I lost my fear of being known as a follower. I had to see Pilate and go into his quarters. I guess I became unclean when I did that. I was remembering how Jesus said that you were not unclean by what you took into your mouth but by what comes out of your mouth. This day was a time of crossroads for both of us. Our lives will never be the same.

(Joseph and Nicodemus freeze.)

Narrator: One of the legends of Joseph was that after the resurrection, at the behest of Peter, Joseph was adopted as one of the 72 disciples. After that he departed for Rome, and was encountered with many hazards on the sea. It is also said that he then went on to Britain to bring the gospel to all.

(Joseph and Nicodemus become animated again.)

Nicodemus: I finally came out of the shadows, too. Why didn't I do this earlier? Maybe it would have made a difference in swaying some of the other members of the Sanhedrin. I thought I was courageous when I said to the others not to rush to judgment about Jesus. Maybe Jesus would not have had to die. Where will all of his followers go?

Joseph: I don't know. It was shameful that more of his followers were not at the crucifixion, but I know they were afraid. John was there with Jesus' mother, Mary, and a few of the other women. But where were the men? I was afraid this afternoon when the earthquake happened along with the darkness and the rain. I wonder if the disciples heard and saw the same things?

Nicodemus: The disciples were afraid, as well they should be. The authorities, Jewish and Roman, will be looking for them. Did you notice a very small stream of water mixed with Jesus' blood? It seemed significant somehow.

(Joseph and Nicodemus freeze.)

Narrator: Both men became bold in witnessing for Jesus' resurrection, but at this particular time, just after his burial, they thought everything was finished.

(Joseph and Nicodemus become animated again.)

Joseph: Nicodemus, do you remember when you first heard and saw Jesus? I ask because I am so glad that you told me about him. If you hadn't, I probably would not have gone to hear him. He truly was the Son of God, and yet, how could he be dead if that is true? Is this the way the Messiah dies?

Nicodemus: I wish I had the answer to that question. About a year ago, I heard that he was teaching around Bethany, so basically I just followed the crowd. I stayed back because I just wanted to listen. I was curious. However, I didn't want to intrude with my clothes indicating that I was a member of the Sanhedrin. What if he really was ... well, you know. I'm sure you felt that way, too, Joseph.

Joseph: Yes, I also wondered if he really could be the Messiah. But I didn't dare say so in the council. Is that the only time you saw Jesus?

Nicodemus: The first time I went by night to see and talk with him. I didn't want to be seen, but I had to talk to him. I told him that I believed that he was a great teacher for all the signs and healings he had done, and he began to tell me that I must be born again! I'm still not sure what that means, because physically it's impossible.

(Joseph and Nicodemus freeze.)

Narrator: Legend has it that Nicodemus was baptized by Peter and John. But then for some reason, he was banned from Jerusalem during the Jewish uprising and the stoning of Stephan. An aprocryphal writing is credited to him, which is simply called, "The Gospel of Nicodemus."

(Joseph and Nicodemus become animated again.)

Joseph: Nicodemus, it seems that we have forsaken our religion by wrapping and burying the crucified body of our Lord. What would you suggest we do now?

Nicodemus: Let's find the disciples and ask to hear their stories and the teachings of Jesus. It would be wonderful to just hear them again. Maybe they have an idea of what we all should do now.

Joseph: Look, Nicodemus! That group of soldiers seems to be coming toward the tomb. Surely they won't disturb the seal!

Nicodemus: I wonder why they want to go to a dead man's tomb?

Lent 5

Innocent Of The Blood Of Jesus

A Monologue
by Joe Barone

Alexander And Rufus: Sons Of Simon Of Cyrene

A Midweek Skit
by Diana M. Morris

Lent 5
Monologue

Innocent Of The Blood Of Jesus
Matthew 27:1-31

Character
  Pontius Pilate

Props
  None required

Setting
  None required

Costume
  Use period costume

Pontius Pilate: He was no threat to the Roman empire, this Jesus. I don't care what they said in their early-morning meeting.

"Are you the King of the Jews?" I asked, and he wouldn't even answer. Oh, they accused him, of course.

The elders and the chief priests, paltry Jewish officials, came before me and accused him.

But what could he do that mattered to me? I was back in Jerusalem at the time — in Fortress Antonia, which overlooked the temple.

It was Passover and the temple was full, but after all, I commanded more than 5,000 men. A lot of them were massed right there.

You had to do that. You had to be ready for disturbances and riots during Passover, but this Jesus was no threat to the Roman empire.

I had complete authority in the province. My only job was to keep Judea for the Roman empire. I didn't care about the Jewish faith. I didn't care about their little meetings and their little leaders. Even now that it's all over, I don't care.

But there's only one thing that bothers me about that time. I was the governor of the province. I was the one who had the right to question witnesses, to sit in the judgment seat, to pass judgment. And I wish I had. In a way, I turned it over to the people. In a way, I let them choose. Oh, I've heard it said that I was a coward, that I was trying to avoid a riot. But that's not the way it happened.

They had their early-morning meeting. They brought him to me, and I failed to decide.

Some day, people may argue about whether it was Jews or Romans who killed Jesus. It was neither. It was the system, the same kind of system of which you're all a part.

Some say he was crucified unjustly. If he was, it wasn't any race or group that killed him. It was human evil, plain and simple. It was human evil struggling to work a human system.

I've heard the stories that he rose again. I've heard the stories that he is the Savior of the world. I've heard it said that when he was born, kings came to worship him, and when he comes again, princes will bow before him.

I've heard all that, but that's not the issue here. The one mistake I made was to wash my hands before the crowd and say, "I'm innocent of this man's blood."

You have to take a stand. No matter who you are, whether you're the governor of the province or a common man, you have to take a stand.

Suppose he did rise again the way they said he did. I may be wrong, but I suspect that if he did, it would have been better to have been the one who killed him than the one who stood aside.

I'd rather be in hell for what I did than what I failed to do.

Let me say that to you again. I'd rather be in hell for what I did than what I failed to do. You can't ignore this Jesus. That's the one thing I learned.

I could have condemned him or freed him, but when I ignored him....

My wife warned me, "Have nothing to do with this righteous man for I have suffered much over him today in a dream." And I just stood aside.

You may think you can stand aside. You may think you can go on about your life, doing whatever it is you want to do.

I've heard the things he said. I've heard the sayings like, "Do not lay up for yourselves treasures on earth, where moth and rust consume and where thieves break in to steal...." Lay up treasures in heaven, he said, and you may think you can ignore that.

I've heard how he said the time would come when he would separate the sheep from the goats based on what they did for the poor, on how they visited the prisoner, and how they helped the hurting. You may think you can ignore that, but I'm here to tell you that this Jesus just keeps coming back.

They say he rose again. They say he is coming to judge the quick and the dead. People are living for him right now and dying for him. I couldn't get away from him. No matter what I did, I couldn't get away from him.

They say he told his disciples to go to all the world and to baptize in the name of "the Father, the Son, and the Holy Spirit," whatever that means. Some of them are trying to do it.

This Jesus just keeps coming back. Oh, I don't believe in him anymore than many so-called Christians do, but I have to think it would have been better for me to have condemned him than to have stepped aside.

There are some things on which you have to take a stand. Like I said before: I'd rather be in hell for something I did than for something I failed to do.

I don't know if you can understand this, but that matters a lot to me right now. I've done a lot of things in my life, but what I failed to do with Jesus may bother me the most.

As I face my own death (and I am about to die), for some reason, I think about this Jesus most of all.

He just keeps coming back.

I was the governor of Judea for ten years, and then just a little while back, I sent troops to break up a riot in the territory of Samaria. The city council of Samaria protested to the governor of Syria, and I was sent to Rome. When I got there, Tiberius, the Roman emperor who was my patron, had died.

I could hardly believe it when I was convicted for malfeasance in my office, and now there's just one honorable thing for me to do.

So I, myself, am facing death. Isn't it odd, that as I face it, I am thinking most of all of Jesus?

Note: We don't know exactly what happened to Pontius Pilate, but according to Christian tradition as Eusebius recorded it, "calamities forced him to unavoidable suicide." He may have killed himself after a trial in Rome during which he was asked to explain the death of several Samaritan fanatics who had gathered at Mount Gerizim to hunt for relics of the prophet Moses.

Lent 5
Midweek Skit

Alexander And Rufus: Sons Of Simon Of Cyrene
Matthew 27:32-37

Characters
    Mother — wife of Simon of Cyrene, mother of Alexander and Rufus, about sixty years of age
    Alexander — about 15 years of age
    Rufus — about 10 years of age

Props
    Chairs

Setting
    Their home in Jerusalem, around 48 AD

Costumes
    All are dressed in common clothes from that time period

(Mother is sitting on a chair, reminiscing about past times. Alexander and Rufus are on the opposite side of the stage.)

Rufus: Father, come back! Come back!

Alexander: Rufus, it will be okay.

Rufus: But where are they taking him? Why did they make him carry that man's crosspiece? Are they going to crucify Father, too?

Alexander: Rufus, come with me and just slip back in the crowd. We'll follow them up to where they are crucifying those men. I think Father is supposed to carry that crosspiece. I'm sure they are not going to hurt him.

(Alexander and Rufus freeze as Mother speaks.)

Mother: I can still hear my sons, telling that story over and over again when they returned to Cyrene with Simon. It's been many, many years ago, and Simon has been gone quite a few years. I know he's with our Lord. Listen again with me, to the story they tell.

(Mother freezes as Alexander and Rufus continue with their story.)

Rufus: I am so frightened! Should we even go to where Father is? Maybe the soldiers will grab us, also. They don't crucify children, do they?

Alexander: Be quiet and just blend in with the people going to see this man, and the two others. What a way to die — such a horrible death. They actually die of suffocation.

Rufus: Don't tell me these things! The things you tell me make me even more nervous.

(Alexander and Rufus freeze as Mother speaks.)

Mother: I felt so sorry for my boys each time I heard them discuss this. I was more sorry for them at the time than for my husband, Simon. And yet, Simon must have been very frightened for himself, carrying that crosspiece. I'm sure he was panicked by having the two boys there, for they were just young men at the time, alone in Jerusalem and wishing he could be with them. Yet, this man was going to die and he was dying in place of that robber and thief, Barabbas. This man looked like he was carrying the weight of the world instead of just a cross. Simon said that when this man looked at him, all he felt was the warmth of love. *(hesitates slightly)* Well, let's go back to listening to my sons' story.

(Mother freezes as Alexander and Rufus continue with their story.)

Rufus: We've been here a while, Alexander, and I still don't see Father. Maybe they are going to crucify him.

Alexander: Don't be ridiculous, Rufus. Father probably has to stay there to help whether he wants to or not. He'll be back with us. But just stay — what was the man saying? I thought I heard him say that he's thirsty. That must be it because they're putting a sponge on a reed.

Rufus: But, he's refusing it! I thought he had said other things, too. Didn't he speak to that woman at the foot of the cross? He's saying something else now even though he can hardly breathe.

Alexander: He said, "It is finished." What does that mean? I suppose I could ask someone.

Rufus: No! You said to blend in and not be noticed. Don't ask anyone. Father might tell us later. Oh look, Alexander, he looks like he's dead. And it's only three o'clock in the afternoon, but it's so dark.

Alexander: That soldier, a Centurion I think, just slid his sword into the man's side. Oh, there is blood and water both coming out. It's so dark, I can't see the cross. The ground is shaking. Now I'm afraid, too, Rufus!

Rufus: But Alexander, before it got so dark and these thunderstorms started, I thought I saw Father up there in back of the group of women. Can we go up that direction to find him?

Alexander: Let's just wait until the wind dies down and the earth quits shaking. Maybe it is Father, but maybe it's someone else.

(Alexander and Rufus freeze as Mother speaks.)

Mother: My sons later told me that the darkness at three o'clock in the afternoon was so frightening because it was like midnight and when the earth was moving and everything shaking because of it, they truly were horrified at the tumult. Then they said it finally started to clear and they were holding on to each other. Then they saw him.

(Mother freezes as Alexander and Rufus continue with their story.)

Rufus: It is Father! Let's go to him. Alexander? *(slowly and thoughtfully)* Alexander? Why are you waiting and looking at that dead man?

Alexander: *(hesitantly)* There is such an expression on his face. There is no agony, no fear. He looks like he is truly at peace. He must have been someone very special.

(Alexander and Rufus freeze as Mother speaks.)

Mother: *(turns away from watching Rufus and Alexander)* Later, Simon found his sons. Simon told them everything that Jesus had said and then he told them about the look and emotion that passed between him and this Jesus. Oh yes, Jesus. Years ago we gave ourselves to him. We knew right from that Sunday morning, or resurrection morning, who he was and that was the beginning of our worship of God through his only Son. *(thoughtfully)* The Son of God — hmmm. The very Son of God that we hold as Lord of our lives. My sons and I believe that Simon, my husband and their father, is with Jesus now. Oh, how I long to see them both — Simon and Jesus!

A few years after Jesus' resurrection, Alexander and Rufus became leaders of Christians in Rome, and then Rufus and Paul became close to each other. God bless us all as we continue to tell the story of Jesus Christ.

Passion/Palm Sunday

Hosanna! Save Now!*

An Introduction and Monologue
by Amy Jo Jones

*This is part one of a three-part monologue series using the same character.

The Monologues for Passion/Palm Sunday, Good Friday, and Easter Day are dedicated first to my parents, Della and the late William L. Jones, who were the first to teach me the stories of Christ.

They are also dedicated to the children of Midlothian United Methodist Church. It is these children who inspired me to write sermons, dramas, and monologues that would capture their attention and imagination. I wrote these monologues while serving that congregation.

— Amy Jo Jones

Passion/Palm Sunday, Good Friday, and Easter Day
Introduction to Monologue Series

Through The Eyes Of A Child

This set of three monologues was inspired by two books: *Crucifixion* by Martin Hengel and *The Upside Down Kingdom* by Donald Kraybill.

Instructions For Use

These monologues portrayed through the eyes of a child are best used as a set, beginning with Palm Sunday and ending on Easter Sunday. However, they can be used separately. The speaker is invited to be creative in the delivery. The speaker should be an adult, assuming the role of being a child. The child can be male or female; hence, the speaker can be male or female. Costuming is at the discretion of each person; however, it is as effective to just assume the role without any kind of visuals or dramatization.

Each one using the monologues is invited to be creative in designing their own worship service around them. Because children (and adults) are visual people, I found that it was quite meaningful to have symbols and visuals at the altar and around the room.

"Hosanna! Save Now!" to be used for Passion/Palm Sunday is found on page 55.

"See How He Died" to be used for Good Friday is found on page 73.

"Do You Believe?" to be used for Easter Day is found on page 131.

Passion/Palm Sunday
Monologue

Hosanna! Save Now!*

Character
This is intended for the pastor to deliver to the congregation.

Music Suggestions For Passion/Palm Sunday
"It Is The Cry Of My Heart"
"We Sing Our Glad Hosannas"
"Hosanna, Loud Hosanna"
"King Of Kings"
"Lord, I Lift Your Name On High"
"All Glory, Laud, And Honor"

Pastor: I know you must find it unusual for a young person to be speaking to you on this high, holy day that you call Palm Sunday. You sometimes sing a hymn called "Hosanna, Loud Hosanna, The Little Children Sang." Please don't think it to be unusual; it's only fitting that a child is here telling you an eternal story.

I want to tell you a story about the first Holy Week from my perspective. Today, I'll tell you about my first Palm Sunday. Actually, in your perspective, it would be the first Palm Sunday ever. Traditions have changed a lot since that first Palm Sunday. Come Good Friday, I'll tell you what it was like to see Jesus die. On Easter, I'll tell you the end — or the true beginning of the story. This story does have a happy ending if you still proclaim to have the hope in resurrection that you say you do. You still proclaim hope in the resurrection, don't you? Good ... I have always known that this is an eternal hope and truth.

"Hosanna" was nothing I sang with joy as much as I sang it in desperation. If you can imagine that words have double meaning, well, "Hosanna" had a double meaning. The first Palm Sunday was not a party — even though we did celebrate on that day. It was a party, a parade, and a cry for help all in one. Things were pretty desperate for us to scream out, "Hosanna!" You know "Hosanna" means "save now." To ask for Jesus to save us immediately, things had to be pretty desperate. "Hosanna" is a cry for help. My dad was about ready to crack under the unfair rules that the temple put on us as a family. I don't think we could have taken another Passover like the ones we had in the past. We were poor and desperate folks.

I was ten years old when I saw Jesus ride into Jerusalem. I was one of the children who ran alongside the donkey and draped my coat over him for Jesus to sit on. Our coats were all we had to prepare the way for our king. I remember how much Jesus really seemed to enjoy having my friends and me run along beside him, and hearing our screams of "Hosanna." He was smiling. But now, when I think about it, I can tell you he had a faraway look in his eyes as if what was happening in the moment did not matter. What we were asking was not a "quick fix" request, even though we wanted Jesus to save us right then. It is hard to tell you everything that happened that day, because I only knew what was going on from a child's point of view.

I can only tell you why I think we were screaming, "Hosanna!" at the top of our lungs. I was with my family on that day. I think you might have heard of my father, Simon.

It was close to Passover, and my family was coming into the temple. We were a poor family from Cyrene. It was difficult for us to celebrate Passover, because each year, when we tried to offer our doves as a sacrifice for the cleansing of our sins, the scribes and Pharisees would tell us that our doves were not perfect, they did not meet the right standards, and they took them from us. They offered us the opportunity to purchase doves that were more "suitable."

Most of the time, we had to go back home because we couldn't afford to buy another dove. I will try to explain it to you in a way that is clearer for today — it would be the same as you being refused forgiveness of your sins because you weren't rich enough to buy forgiveness when you came to church. I did not like the way things were run in the temple because it did not seem to be fair. I thought God's forgiveness was offered to all, not just to those who could afford to buy it. I did not like what it did to my family for us to be turned away from the temple. When the ritual of sacrifice for forgiveness cannot be done from one year to the next, some begin to think that they are unforgiven and worthless. We were certainly treated that way. I was taught that true religion is what freed us to love God and our neighbor that opposed the way we felt each time we left the temple. We felt like we had to earn, as well as, buy God's forgiveness.

I remember my family singing a psalm that made sense to us especially when we could not go through the ritual of yearly sacrifices ... "You do not delight in sacrifice, or I would bring it; you do not take pleasure in burnt offerings. The sacrifices of God are a broken spirit: a broken and contrite heart. O God, you will not despise." It seemed that all we ever had to offer God was a broken and contrite heart. That is Psalm 51, and we knew it as a psalm that we sang, knowing that God looked at our hearts and not at how much we had, or did not have. I don't think God expected us to be rich to go to the temple. I don't think Jesus expected us to be, either. Our only lifeline of knowing that we were not despicable people was that God did not despise our broken and contrite hearts.

I think the religious leaders expected us to be rich. One year, I remember that we were able to purchase a dove and we were pleased that we could afford it. We did not have to hang our heads and go home. They had taken our doves from us to begin with because they were not perfect enough — in their opinion. I knew this was going to happen. They did this every year. I remember that I had made a small mark in the beak of one of our doves — not so you could see or anything, but one that only I knew was there — and wouldn't you know it, we were sold the same dove that we were told was not good enough! We purchased our own dove — the one we had just given to them! That dove had the same mark on his beak because I put it there. We were ripped off. I was so furious! And there was nothing I could do. I was just a child. The religious leaders were doing this to everyone. They were putting us in a powerless position where we had no voice. Pardon me for saying this, but I didn't think religion was supposed to do that to anyone. At least they were doing this to everyone, not just my family. I can understand why Jesus was so furious when he went in and overturned the tables. He knew what was going on, too. I can understand why he called them a den of thieves because that was what temple was to me. I don't want to get ahead of myself, though ... because he had not yet gone into the temple to cleanse it on the day we paraded into Jerusalem. However, I was sure that his cleansing of the temple was a part of our cries for help being heard. He was saving us. At least he could fly into a holy rage and get away with it. The religious leaders already thought he was crazy — and he broke all of their rules.

I tell you all these things about the religious leaders of my time because when it came to the yearly rituals of forgiveness and cleansing of our hearts before the altar of God, if we were not able to participate, we were cast out and treated as scum. It was very important for us to participate in this, as a community and as a family. We wanted to be accepted. We would be seen as unforgiven and unforgivable. There were a lot of us who were treated like scum. It was almost as if there was a whole community of people who were considered to be the filth and scum of the earth, and yet what had we done? We were just poor, and we were deliberately kept that way from what I could see. I mean, what government strips its citizens of their belongings and then turns around and sells that same property back to them at an outrageous price? Isn't that deliberate oppression? Is religion supposed to be an oppressive power? I thought true religion was supposed to allow people to be free to love God and their neighbors.

Things were pretty horrible for my family and for families like mine. We needed Jesus. We were desperate. What we needed was Jesus to save us right then. Hosanna! Save us! Save us now! NOW! Hosanna! This was not some selfish thing we were asking for. I knew that Jesus loved me. I knew that he cared for me. I knew that he loved the poor. I knew that he also had connections to those in the temple who treated us like dirt and that he showed them the same kind of love he showed us. Maybe he could do something. Maybe he could save us. We started to chant, "Hosanna!" We chanted it with determination and conviction. We chanted it at the top of our lungs.

All of us gathered around Jesus like you see the team gathering around a coach, carrying him on their shoulders. I think we would have put him on our shoulders, but Jesus rode in on a donkey, sitting upon my coat. There were hoards of us running and screaming, "Save us now — Hosanna!" Can you hear the crowds in your mind? Can you hear what I was a part of? If you can imagine the crowd at a football game ... you can imagine the loud chanting of Hosanna. It was a party, a parade, and a cry for help all in one. We had such hope that Jesus could save us. We had such hope that Jesus could overthrow our religious government and make it into something more bearable. That's what the parade was about. We thought we had a king. We were a crowd big enough to overthrow the religious government if we only had a king who would take our side. Jesus had to be our king. This parade was nothing like I had ever seen before.

I know you all know the end of this story. But, sometimes it's important to hear what it was about then. We weren't thinking of 2,000 years ahead, we were thinking of what our immediate needs were. When I think of what we were trying to do with Jesus on that day, we were looking for a quick fix. We were looking for relief from a problem that ran much deeper than making Jesus a king in the same way you would elect a president. We wanted our problems to go away. "Save us now" was really our cry for help, our cry for a quick fix, and our cry to be delivered from poverty. I think that is the way I understood it. That is why we formed such a crowd around Jesus and we were ready to have an inauguration on the same day. That is not what Jesus had in mind, however. Jesus was not really about taking sides as much as he was interested in a level playing field for all. Jesus wanted the oppressed to love the oppressor, and he wanted the oppressors to love the oppressed — love would erase the levels of class and hierarchy, and all would be seen as equal and loved children of God. Jesus had a better plan. You will see that in time, as I tell you my story.

I don't know if you can hear, "Hosanna" any differently now that I have told you about the desperate circumstances. But I hope that you can hear that same cry from people like me today. Can you hear the cries of the poor and the oppressed? Can you hear the cries of the outcasts and the people your society treats as scum? Can you hear the cries of those who are deliberately turned into scapegoats? "Hosanna" is a cry of desperation by people who are in pain, whose only hope is in God. Perhaps Jesus wanted everyone to cry, "Hosanna" because he simply wanted everyone to realize that their only hope was in God. The oppressed and the oppressors only have one hope. Have you cried this prayer to Jesus? Have you been so desperate to cry, "Save us now"?

I've wondered about this desperation cry ... that perhaps it is time for the church to cry this cry again, at the top of its lungs. Hosanna! I've wondered if this could even be the cry of your heart? I go from church to church every year telling this story. Is there the same sense of desperation for Jesus to save you now? Can you imagine what it was like for me? Can you join the crowd that I'm a part of and start chanting, "Hosanna"? Can you take the same journey with me?

Palm branches and all of these things that we laid out on the road to prepare the way for the Lord, those were only symbols. Today, I would tell you to treat yourself as a garment or as palm branches to be spread under Christ's feet as he enters in.

I have so much more to tell you about this week, but, I'll tell you on Friday. I want to tell you my whole story of who Jesus is to me. Take this journey with me.

*This is part one of a three-part monologue series using the same character.

Maundy Thursday

The Eyes Of Jesus

An Introduction, Worship Service, and Monologue
by Amy Jo Jones

We Worship You

A Litany
by Jeff Milsten

This worship service is dedicated to the memory of my father, William L. Jones, who was a true example of what it means to be a servant of God.

— Amy Jo Jones

Maundy Thursday
Introduction

The Eyes Of Jesus

It is suggested that those who serve in positions of leadership take part in this worship service. The idea behind this is to illustrate the model of servant leadership. This service can be adapted and designed for any congregation's particular use. I have not included a communion liturgy for this purpose; each congregation is invited to adapt their own traditional liturgies for Maundy Thursday.

During Holy Communion and the Foot Washing, it is suggested that the church council or administrative council take part in serving Holy Communion and having their feet washed and washing feet. Depending upon the size of the congregation, it is suggested that the pastor and the church leaders serve as those who will wash the feet of the congregants. Communion is best done by intinction, with a single-file line, followed by several foot washing stations in the front and along the sides of the sanctuary — depending upon the architectural design of the sanctuary. After the pastor has consecrated the elements, the pastor will serve the servers, who will then, in turn, serve the pastor. The pastor will also wash the servers' feet, who, in turn, will wash the pastor's feet. The pastor will then depart from the table and be stationed at a designated place to wash the feet of the congregation. This part of the service should be done in silence.

The Stripping Of The Church

The stripping of the church service has been adapted from "From Ashes To Fire," in *Supplemental Worship Resources 8: Services of Worship for the Seasons of Lent and Easter*, published by Abingdon Press, Nashville, 1979. The stripping of the church dates from the seventh century and was designed to be a useful service of cleansing and washing the church in preparation for Easter Sunday.

As a part of the stripping of the church, it is suggested that the only things that remain on the altar following this ritual are a basin, a towel, and the pastor's stole. The stole is symbolic of the towel Christ used to wash the disciples' feet.

Organization of this part of the worship service works best if many people are involved — including (and especially) children. Each person will remove one assigned item from the sanctuary, in single file. The last item to be removed is the Christ Candle, still illuminated. On Easter Sunday, the same people will bring in the items that were removed, including the decoration of the church as a part of the processional and the worship service. For those congregations who arrange the flowers and decorate the sanctuary on Saturday, it is suggested to keep the decorations to a minimum, and include the flowers as a part of the procession, thus allowing the decoration of the sanctuary to be a part of the worship service on Easter Sunday. More people may be needed on Easter Sunday if it is decided that the flower decorations are a part of the processional. Discretion is advised.

Suggested Music
"The Basin And The Towel" by Michael Card
"Jesu, Jesu"
"Turn Your Eyes Upon Jesus"
"The Summons"

Suggested Music During Communion
"Help Us Accept Each Other"
"Now, Now"
"I Have Decided To Follow Jesus"
"In Remembrance Of Me"
"Let Us Be Bread"

Maundy Thursday
Worship Service

The Eyes Of Jesus
(Includes Holy Communion, Foot Washing, and The Stripping Of The Church)

Prelude "The Basin And The Towel"
by Michael Card

Greeting
    This evening, we come together, being stripped of all pretense and arrogance as we seek to become closer to Christ. May this be a time of self-examination and relinquishing all control as we seek to be clothed with Christ.

Call To Worship (based on Psalm 116)
Leader: How shall we return to the Lord for all his goodness to us?
All: **We will lift up the cup of salvation and call upon the name of the Lord.**
Leader: We will pay our vows to the Lord
All: **in the presence of all God's people.**
Leader: We are your servants, you have freed us to love without condition.
All: **We will offer you the sacrifice of our lives and call on you at all times.**
Leader: We will pay our vows to the Lord.
All: **We will pay our vows to you, in the midst of all your people. Praise the Lord!**

Opening Hymn "Jesu, Jesu"

Prayer Of Confession *(in unison)*
    Holy God, we lay bare our souls before you this night. We come before you with our hearts opened in order to be cleansed, and to find our true selves in your presence. We confess that we have become arrogant, presuming to possess Jesus rather than to embrace him. We confess that we have used Jesus as an idol and as a defense rather than having embraced him as our companion. We have failed to share his life with others. We have failed to serve as he has served us. Forgive us. Let your grace penetrate our hearts and cleanse us, revealing to us the very nature of who you want us to be. In Jesus' name. Amen.

Gospel Lesson John 13:1-17, 31b-35

Meditation "The Eyes Of Jesus"

Hymn "Turn Your Eyes Upon Jesus"

Service Of Holy Communion And Foot Washing

Hymn "The Summons"

The Stripping Of The Church *(to be done in silence)*

Benediction

Now service begins. Go into the world in the knowledge that we are Christ's body, that hope for a new world is in the blood of our veins, and that God's promise is the very stuff of which our bones are wrought.

The grace of our Lord Jesus Christ, the love of God, and the communion of the Holy Spirit, be with us all, today and always. Amen.

Postlude

Maundy Thursday
Monologue

The Eyes Of Jesus

Character
This is intended for the pastor to deliver to the congregation.

Pastor: It's been 2,000 years since I first looked into the eyes of Jesus ... I mean ... *really* looked. It's a day I will never forget. I remember that night as if it were yesterday. I remember everything that I was feeling. I remember....

As I watched Jesus quietly make his rounds, washing feet, I started to get nervous. I wonder if any of the other disciples caught what he was doing when he started that task. He was so unobtrusive in his actions and demeanor. My fingers were tapping on the table. I kept crossing and uncrossing my legs. I kept tapping my toes, and my legs were so hyperactive that I could have run five miles without even breathing hard. Everything about my body language was hyper and nervous. My heart was racing. I kept clearing my throat. I tend to get nervous when things get personal. I say the wrong things, stumble over my thoughts, and fight against the desire to flee the scene. You know how it goes when you get nervous and jittery. You want to leave and stay at the same time. I resolved not to let my nerves take over and prevent me from what I knew I needed to experience. My heart was burning and racing as Jesus drew closer.

Jesus seemed to be so calm and so thoroughly engrossed in what he was doing, that he did not seem to notice anyone in the room except for the person he was tending to at the time. Sometimes I wondered if he even noticed the person; he seemed intent on washing our feet and doing nothing else. Time seemed to stop when he was tending to each individual. As I was watching him, there was a moment in which the only thing that existed in the room was just he and myself, as I watched him wash Peter's feet and heard his argument with Jesus. I was mesmerized by what I was seeing, even though I was so nervous.

There was a mystery about what I was seeing. Normally, I never noticed foot washing; it was something slaves did. Slaves were never noticed except when they failed to meet the expectations of the master. However, I kept watching this man, whom I knew to have all things put under him ... he was using his hands of authority and majesty and a servant's towel and basin to do a slave's job. His hands moved with compassion, love, and as if he was touching the deepest parts of our souls simply by washing our feet. Nothing else seemed to exist to him except that one simple task of washing a person's feet. I was in awe.

My mind went into a whirlwind of questions. Why? How? What does this mean? What was I to do? I watched Jesus when he wasn't looking at me. I couldn't take my eyes off him. Sometimes our eyes would meet and he held my gaze. I had not yet learned that eye contact with Jesus is the most important thing that exists in my relationship with him. I had to see what he was doing. I had to look. I had something to learn, I could feel it. I knew I was going to have to look Jesus in the eyes as he washed my feet, and let him hold me with his eyes for me to learn what I needed to learn. Whatever he needed to teach me, I knew that it was going to be a wordless exchange. I had to listen to him with my eyes, the eyes of my heart. I needed to perceive what I was seeing — ever seeing and never perceiving — he said something like that. I really wanted to perceive what he was doing. I wanted to listen to his heart and hear and see what he was teaching me through his heart.

While I was waiting for my turn in this, I began to take inventory of my spirit and soul. I had become so proud to be one of his followers! I realized that I had exalted him and turned him into an idol. He had become an idol of pride. I was "proud" to follow him. He made me feel like I was worth something, had something to offer, and could do anything, just by following him. I felt like a person of worth because I was and I am. However, my pride had turned into exclusiveness and I was immediately confronted with the exclusivity of the Pharisee within my spirit. I had an idolatrous pride. I had become so arrogant. I had become a snob. I had become greedy and eager to be noticed because I had given in to arrogant behavior. I had become someone no one really liked because of it. I had so much I needed to learn. My feelings of pompous pride faded as I watched Jesus show me some deep things, just by his actions. I imagined feeling Jesus' hands on my feet before he got to me. Who was this man who was going to wash my feet? What was he going to teach me? Why was he doing that?

He was showing me how to serve, how to love, and how to be loved. However, I could only see that his love was something that I sought to own and keep in my own life. I wanted to hoard him — like owning a house, owning a boat, and owning stock. I was not going to share what I had been given. I was watching myself turn into an arrogant person, prideful, and with walls around me because there was no way I was going to give away what I had discovered. It was mine to keep. My possessiveness and clinginess turned into the trap in which I fell. Possessiveness clamped my spirit like the jaws of an animal trap. The more I pulled, the tighter I was trapped. I wanted to be the greatest in his eyes. I wanted to be his favorite. Can you see the vicious cycle in which I was trapped?

I was so nervous when he came to me. He looked me in the eyes. I forgot my nerves as he held my eyes with his. I was mesmerized by his gaze. I could not move. His eyes began to empower me to relinquish the possessiveness. His love was mine. But I could not own him anymore than he owned me. It was as if he could see straight through me, down into the soles of my feet. I could feel his eyes following me as I continued to do inventory. I could feel his eyes penetrating my soul, searching me, inviting me into a deeper relationship. I wanted to know what he was thinking and feeling as he was washing my feet, as he was living within that moment. I could feel his eyes loving me, embracing me, and simply holding me.

I could not take my eyes off him. You know how you get into that zone where you become so focused on something that even your peripheral vision doesn't exist? That was the kind of focus I had on Jesus. I could not take my eyes off him. I realized how much I loved him, how much he loved me, and that he was treating me with such worth through this one little event of washing my feet. When his hands touched my feet for the first time, my heart melted; I felt like he was touching my heart instead of my feet.

My idolatrous pride, which I had thought to be stone, crumbled like clay. I was left as naked as the day I was born, to reflect upon a Savior who literally had become nothing and was treating me as somebody. His hands were loving me and serving me and teaching me. His eyes were embracing me, healing my soul, and filling me with light. I know this is what Jesus wanted to give me: enough love for me to be able to let go of every preconceived prejudice and idolized notion of what it meant to follow him in order that he could teach me what it really meant to serve him and to let his light into my soul. He washed my feet.

Jesus was teaching me to give up all security in order to be secure in him just by touching my feet and looking into my eyes. I've replayed this night over and over in my mind. I have felt him pouring water over my feet again and again. I realized later how vulnerable I had become in his presence. I realized how secure I was in his presence to be vulnerable. I knew that being vulnerable with him, I could afford to show that vulnerability to others around me, to let them know of the deep love our Savior has for all of us.

It's not what I felt physically. It was in watching him and in him watching me. It was a wordless exchange. No one really saw what was taking place between us in that moment. All you would have seen had you been there, is a man stooping to wash my feet with me watching his every move. You would have seen us looking at each other. But you would not have heard the exchange that was taking place between his spirit and my spirit unless you listened with your heart. He held my eyes for what seemed like an eternity. I still see his eyes as our eyes met each other then. He looked at me with such intent. He looked at me with such great depth and intensity. I saw compassion. I saw patience. I saw determination. I saw encouragement. I saw the longing in his eyes mixed with love. Just by his eyes looking into my eyes, I felt embraced, taught, and encouraged. I felt healed and forgiven. There was such intimacy and intensity in what Jesus was inviting me into.

This experience has caused me to reflect. He serves me, even today. He doesn't serve me to my beck and call. I can't just magically call upon him, snap my fingers, and expect him to do for me like a slave would do. I'm not the master. He's the Master. He's also the servant. He serves me as a means to nurture me. Jesus was showing me that servants are nurturing people, not asking for any recognition. It was such a low-profile event. Washing feet and looking people in the eye — these were really simple things that were so hard for me to grasp. Serving others as a part of following Jesus did not mean that I could be controlled by others' whims — at least not in the way I learned from this. Servants meet needs and know what those needs are. He continues to serve me to show me how to serve. He shows me how to be a nurturing person and he nurtures me. There is connection in this serving. There is such a connection to Jesus in learning how to serve this way.

I'm not able to look into your eyes in the same manner he looked into mine. I'm not able to hold the gaze and the searching look as much as I would like to with you. I am still learning to look at Jesus. It scares me because of the great vulnerability that the Savior has called us all into with each other. It has taken me 2,000 years to begin to put this together and to understand the depth and nature of the Savior's call and example to me. I hope that some day I can serve you with complete abandonment to the extent that it does not matter what you think of me, but that I can serve you in order that we can share in servanthood with each other. We are called to serve to the same depth and capacity and intimacy with which Jesus has served us and serves us still.

Maundy Thursday
Litany

We Worship You

Leader: Let us remember and never forget.
People: If your only act of love had been to create the universe,
Leader: it would have been enough to worship you, God.
People: If your only act of love had been to create people, male and female,
Leader: it would have been enough to worship you, God.
People: If your only act of love had been to keep in faithful relationship,
Leader: it would have been enough to worship you, God.
People: If your only act of love had been to save Israel from slavery and give freedom,
Leader: it would have been enough to worship you, God.
People: If your only act of love had been to form Israel as your example for the world,
Leader: it would have been enough to worship you, God.
People: If your only act of love had been giving us scriptural guidance for better living life,
Leader: it would have been enough to worship you, God.
People: If your only act of love had been to come to us in humility and love in Jesus,
Leader: it would have been enough to worship you, God.
People: If your only act of love had been to give us Jesus as your example of your love and teacher of how we are to be,
Leader: it would have been enough to worship you, God.
People: If your only act of love had been to die for us in Jesus,
Leader: it would have been enough to worship you, God.
People: If your only act of love had been Jesus' resurrection and our hope,
Leader: it would have been enough to worship you, God.
People: If your only acts of love had been your continued presence holding us together, miracles, touchstone experiences, and daily actions for us,
Leader: it would have been enough to worship you, God.
People: If your only act of love had been your inspiring so many people through history to change our lives for the better,
Leader: it would have been enough to worship you, God.
People: You, dear God — Father, Son, and Holy Spirit, have done all this and more. Thank you.
Leader: Let us remember and never forget.

Good Friday

See How He Died*

A Monologue
by Amy Jo Jones

All Are Worthy

A Play
by Joseph M. Beer

*This is part two of a three-part monologue series using the same character.

Good Friday
Monologue

See How He Died*

Character
This is intended for the pastor to deliver to the congregation.

Music Suggestions For Good Friday
"Watch The Lamb" by Ray Boltz (This song, in particular, inspired the monologue for Good Friday.)
"Why" by Michael Card
"To Mock Your Reign, O Dearest Lord"
"Were You There?"
"What Wondrous Love Is This?"
"When I Survey The Wondrous Cross"

Pastor: I haven't aged much since that night in Jerusalem. I've been wandering around this earth, visiting from place to place, and still feeling as terrified as I felt 2,000 years ago. There's just so much violence, blood, and guts in this world. I see it every day wherever I go, and it still terrifies me as much as the first time I saw violence. Can we ever get a grip on ourselves as a whole and stop killing one another?

I saw violence for the first time to three other human beings 2,000 years ago. One in particular I remember well, because he was my friend. I was ten years old when I saw my friend die a violent, bloody, and ugly death. Have you ever seen someone die an unjust, violent death? You can't forget it. To see it repeated throughout history is excruciating.

I was with my parents. We were coming to Jerusalem to celebrate Passover. We always came from Cyrene every year to celebrate the Passover. My parents told me that my responsibility was to take care of the lamb that would be sacrificed, and we would later eat is as a part of our meal.

I had a different pet lamb every year and I loved them all. We all took care of this lamb and made sure he didn't get hurt. He had to be perfect in order to sacrifice him. I used to carry him and cuddle him wherever he would go, and he would often nuzzle his face against mine, and I would feel his soft wool against me. I loved this lamb. I hugged him all the time. It was hard work to take care of this lamb in Jerusalem because Jerusalem became crowded, and there were many children just like me taking care of our lambs. I sure hoped I didn't get mine mixed up with anyone else's. I kept mine next to me, tied up with a rope around its neck — but not too tightly for fear of rope burn. I had a very important job to do. I hated to see my lamb die every year. I hated it. I cried every time my lamb died. It was hard to eat him but it was tradition and I had to do it. We did this every year at the same time. I always asked why we had to do this, why we had to kill a lamb. My parents would tell me the same story every year, how it was a remembrance of God's love and care for us all, how he took care of us. I didn't get it. If God took care of us and saved us, then why did my lamb always have to die every year? It made no sense ... but my parents seemed to understand it, so I thought that maybe some day I would understand when I was older. Maybe that is why it was my job to ask the same question every year: "Why do we do this?"

It was so crowded! A week ago, we had just finished being in a parade where we celebrated Jesus riding into Jerusalem on a donkey. We were sure he was going to be our king. It was strange, because I never remembered a parade like that before. I didn't understand it all, but he sure looked pleased when I gave him my coat to sit on as I draped it over the donkey. He smiled at me and tussled my hair and sent me off. I felt so loved by Jesus. I felt so important to him because he seemed to care about everything that I did.

I was the one you have read about in your Bibles. I was the one he brought to himself and he taught his disciples about how important I was. He told them that it would be better for a millstone to be tied around their necks and for them to be tossed into the sea rather than cause me to sin. I thought that was really cool! Even I could imagine seeing people with millstones around their necks and sinking in the sea. Jesus really cared about me. He took me seriously and joyfully at the same time. I knew it. I knew that he loved me. He loved my friends, too. I always noticed that he played with all of us children as if he were a big child himself, and then he taught the adults. I thought it was supposed to be the other way around. He was always laughing around us, playing silly games, and wrestling with us. I loved it! He was the only adult in my life who treated me like a real person and made me think that everything I did was really important. I really loved Jesus! I wanted to devote my entire life to him because of his love for me.

That's why I got so confused on the night of the Passover. At first, I thought it was another parade, but the crowd was different. They were screaming some hoodlum's name — Barabbas. I had heard of him. He was an awful man. My parents were not at all pleased when they heard he was being released. At first, we thought he was going to be crucified, but then I saw him running away from the entire crowd, with a smirk on his face. I cowered behind my mother. I started to get scared. This was different from any Passover I remembered.

We were on our way to the temple, getting ready to sacrifice our lamb, and we got caught in an angry mob of people going up the hill where they executed people. We couldn't escape. Everybody was yelling, "Crucify him! Crucify him!" Bloody murder was in the sound of their voices. They were going to that place I had heard about, but was not allowed to see. My parents wanted to shelter me from all of that. There were so many bones lying around in that yard that it had been nicknamed the Skull, but I believe it was really named Golgotha. The thought of all those bones sent chills through my body, because I knew that they were not bones from animals. They were human bones.

I saw three men carrying crosses. Two of them were completely naked, but the other one was so bloody, I could not tell if he was dressed or not. I was so scared. I was frightened. I was terrified. I wanted to scream at what I was seeing. But the scream was trapped in my throat, and tears were running down my face. I was clinging to my mother. I was hiding behind her and crying. I was terrified.

I kept peeking through my tears, because I thought I knew the bloody man. He was so weak. He kept falling with that heavy cross. All of a sudden, I recognized him! It was Jesus! It was Jesus! Why him? I started to cry again. What had Jesus done? Jesus was my friend. Jesus loved me. I knew that he did. I loved him. Why was this happening? How could these people not see that he was a great man and one of the best friends anyone could have?

I forgot where I was for a moment and I let go of my mom. This was wrong. I wanted to stop it and save Jesus. I ran up through the crowd and went up to Jesus. I guess I was like one of those children who bolt from their parents, because I heard my daddy cry out to me and start after me. My mother stayed with my brother and sister. I almost got to Jesus. I wanted so badly to hold on to him and hug him and scream at those ugly people to leave Jesus alone. He had done nothing wrong. He was my best friend. They kept hitting him with whips and spitting on him. His back was bleeding so badly that it looked like a piece of raw meat. His face was so bloody, and I didn't realize why until I saw this thorny wreath around his head.

I cried so hard. I was scared and I shrieked. They were getting ready to kill Jesus! Why? Jesus, my only friend in the world who treated me like I was somebody, who treated me like I was important. Until Jesus touched me and held me, I had always felt so invisible. Jesus made me feel like the most important person in his life when we were together. Why were they getting ready to kill him? I wanted to save him. I tried. I really tried. I was screaming, "Jesus, Jesus!" when I was running to save him.

My daddy caught up with me and grabbed me by my collar before I could touch Jesus. Jesus saw me. He gave me a look that said he would be okay, but, I didn't get it at the time. I knew that he heard me call his name, though. It was so hard to see that look, that he would be okay, through the tears running down my face and the shrieks coming from deep within my heart. I was so scared for Jesus. I didn't want to see this. I had never seen anything die except the sacrificial lamb, and I always cried. I didn't want to see Jesus die. Not this way.

Daddy caught me and sent me back to Mommy. When the soldiers saw how close Daddy was to Jesus, they grabbed him. I shrieked because I thought they were going to kill Daddy, too. But yet, I heard one of the soldiers holler, "Hey, Simon!" (That was my daddy's name.) "Hey, you, Simon, carry this cross for this ..." I would rather not tell you the awful name they called Jesus because I am not allowed to repeat it.

Daddy carried the cross up to that hill with all the bones all over it, and Jesus walked alongside of him ... or crawled. Jesus stumbled a lot. I was glad that, in some way, I could help Jesus. Maybe my running away from my parents and toward him is what I did to help him.

I had never seen an execution before, but I had heard about them. I just couldn't believe it was happening to Jesus. It just didn't seem right. I couldn't believe that they were doing this on the night that my daddy had always told me that we remembered how God saved us. It was bad enough that my lamb had to die a terrible death, but it was even worse to watch this happen.

My friend, Jesus, was being killed. My heart was breaking in two. I could not understand. I could not understand the violence then, and I can't understand it today. Jesus loved me. I loved Jesus. He told me that I needed to love others because of his love for me. It was such a simple thing. That's why I could understand him. He always made things so simple for me to understand.

I heard the hammers as they nailed stakes through Jesus' hands and feet to hold him on the cross. I screamed! I screamed with Jesus as he screamed in pain. I was so close to this whole thing, that I could see the tears running down Jesus' face through the blood. He was suffering so badly.

They stripped Jesus. His whole body was covered with blood. His body was soaked in blood, and he was naked. I had heard that the worst thing that they could do to a Jewish man was to strip him in public and then kill him. What was I seeing? Jesus didn't deserve this at all! Why was this happening?

They raised that cross and dropped it into the ground. I saw Jesus' bloody body jerk and shake, and his flesh rip around the nails as he was jarred. He screamed. He screamed so loudly in pain.

I was crying so hard. My heart was breaking in two. I wanted to save Jesus. Everyone was making fun of him, spitting on him, and mocking him. I couldn't do it. I didn't want my friend to die. He was my best grown-up friend. In fact, he was the best grown-up friend any child had. I didn't want to see this. How could they do this to my friend?

I watched Jesus' ribs and chest labor to breathe. Some of the soldiers gave him something really bitter to drink. I saw Jesus look at his mother. He was concerned about her, and he made sure she was taken care of. I saw him scream at God. I saw him talk to the two criminals on his right and left.

He kept laboring to breathe. His breathing had a death rattle about it. It was as if he was struggling to live and to die at the same time. The cross was covered with blood. His face, his hands, his back ... all were so bloody that none of us could hardly recognize him. The blood reminded me of the blood of the sacrifice when all those lambs were killed. Jesus was bleeding to death and suffocating. He was suffering so badly.

I watched Jesus die. I had never seen anybody die before. I had seen my lambs killed. I had not seen a person die. Jesus screamed aloud and said, "It is accomplished!" It was as if he was being ripped from this world, and he died. Jesus' body quit moving completely, his ribs and chest stopped moving, and he dangled from the cross. He was dead. My friend was dead. I was crying, my parents were crying. Jesus' disciples were crying.

I forgot to tell you, I lost my lamb. My lamb ran away from the angry mob. The only comfort I had was that my lamb did not die that year, but my friend, Jesus, died. I will never forget this Passover. Why does something always have to die in order that we will remind ourselves that God loves and cares for us? That question has yet to be answered. All I knew was that Jesus was dead. My best friend was dead. I cried myself to sleep. My parents couldn't explain this one to me. Jesus was their friend, too, and he was dead. Would any of this ever make any sense?

*This is part two of a three-part monologue series using the same character.

Good Friday
Play

All Are Worthy

Characters
    Zerah
    Jude
    Judas
    Simon
    Miriam
    Abigail
    Jesus (offstage voice)

Props
    Table
    Chairs
    Furniture
    Bowl of food
    Bowl of fruit
    Plates
    Silverware

Setting
    Scene One: home of Zerah, outside of Jericho
    Scene Two: home of Miriam and Abigail in Capernaum, a few weeks later
    Scene Three: synagogue courtyard in Capernaum
    Scene Four: at the cross
    Scene Five: somewhere in Jerusalem, the next day

Costumes
    Use period costumes

Scene One
The home of Zerah, outside of Jericho
(As the lights come up, Zerah is sitting. Simon, Judas, and Jude enter.)

Zerah: Welcome, my sons. Come, sit and drink. I have been waiting to hear your news.

Jude: Thank you, Rabbi Zerah.

Judas: We always appreciate your hospitality. *(sits)*

Simon: Master Zerah, you have taught us so much over the years. Besides teaching us to be stonemasons, you have taught us the law of God.

Zerah: Working with God's creation makes one with his laws.

Judas: Our work also allows us the freedom to move about Palestine.

Jude: We find out how other Jews are observing the law and dealing with our enemies the Romans.

Simon: Master, we find so many Jews not observing the laws of the Torah.

Zerah: That is why the Romans rule us. I have always taught you that we must deal harshly with the ungodly and our Gentile enemies.

Judas: But, we are only stonemasons. We cannot fight every ungodly person and the Romans. We need an army of zealous Jews in order to prevail.

Zerah: I have prayed for God to send us a leader who will gather all who are zealous for his law to convince our people to turn back to God.

Simon: And, we are not leaders?

Zerah: You are zealous, but, no, you are not leaders.

Jude: Master, you are a leader. Why don't you lead us? We will help you gain followers like Judas of Galilee, who taught you the Zealot way.

Zerah: I am too old, and I never had the charisma of Judas of Galilee. He had a gift for leading that God only bestows on a select few.

Judas: Like the great King David and Moses?

Zerah: Yes. I tried to carry on the work of your namesake after they killed him, but I was not the speaker he was. I can teach, but I do not have the gift he had.

Simon: Neither do we.

Zerah: Correct. That is why I encourage you to go throughout the country in the hope that you will find the one I pray for.

Judas: Yet, we have not found that person. I believe God has abandoned us because our people pervert the law instead of embracing it.

Jude: And, if one does rise up, our leaders or the Romans will eliminate them like they did Judas of Galilee.

Zerah: You must not say that. We will be delivered just as our ancestors were from Egypt.

Jude: *(stands and crosses)* When? Judas of Galilee failed and no one has arisen to rid us of the Roman yoke.

Zerah: *(moves toward the table)* It will happen when our people turn back to God and his law.

Simon: *(stands)* Jude, Master Zerah has taught us that it is our job to educate our fellow Jews. We are to convince them to purify themselves and turn to God.

Jude: And how successful have we been? Everywhere we work we try and are laughed at for believing God's law will deliver us.

Simon: We have turned some back to God. We have convinced many in our profession to purify themselves as well as others in Galilee.

Judas: But, we need a leader to bring all Jews together.

Zerah: Judas is right. You have been good at bringing some back to the law, but more must come to God before the deliverer will come.

Simon: How do you know?

Zerah: *(sits)* That is what God has revealed to these old eyes. So, please tell me about this Baptist fellow. I have heard he has a powerful message.

Simon: *(crosses)* He preaches repentance like we and others have.

Judas: He does not seem educated in the Torah.

Jude: He looks like a wild man, but people flock to him. No one has baptized so many. He may not know all the law, as you say, but I thought he was charismatic.

Zerah: Can he lead our people against the enemy? Can he bring them back to God?

Jude: That is what he is doing. He teaches them they must repent of their sins.

Zerah: You said that. Others have done that. What I want to know is if you think he could gather an army to face the Romans.

Judas: *(pauses)* Master Zerah, the Baptist attracts all sorts of outcasts.

Simon: Tax collectors, prostitutes, even the homeless come to be baptized.

Jude: But, if the Baptist can make them more zealous for God, that is good.

Zerah: Tax collectors are flunkies for the Romans. They are not worthy of being called Jews. Judas of Galilee taught me that paying taxes is an abomination to God. God is the only one we owe.

Jude: Do not our leaders in Jerusalem also do Rome's bidding?

Zerah: They, too, need to be dealt with. That is why I prayed God will send his Messiah to purge our nation of the Romans and collaborators like the Maccabeans did.

Simon: We all hope and pray for this, but we have heard many false messiahs. That is why I am no longer sure God will send his Messiah.

Zerah: *(stands)* Never say that. God will send his Messiah. Of that I am sure.

Judas: We need a Messiah who can gather an armed force to march on Jerusalem in order to rid ourselves of Rome.

Jude: They are experienced warriors. That is why they rule us.

Simon: Master, you have created a network of zealous Jews throughout Palestine, maybe one of them could lead us; one who could lead as Judas of Galilee did.

Zerah: *(moves to center and around table)* Judas of Galilee was not a Messiah. He led a tax revolt, not a national revolution.

Jude: What does paying taxes have to do with the law?

Judas: Where in the Torah does it say we are to pay taxes to an occupying army?

Zerah: I told you it is an abomination. Paying taxes is like offering sacrifices to an idol.

Simon: Yet, we do it to survive.

Zerah: What does the Baptist tell the tax collectors to do?

Simon: Do not collect more than is legal.

Zerah: *(sits)* That's it?

Judas: He did not tell them they were violating the law. He cannot be considered a Zealot leader.

Jude: But, he preaches repentance and is successful. Is that not being zealous for God? Is that not leading?

Zerah: Does he have many disciples?

Simon: Yes. They help the people down to the water and give food to anyone who needs it.

Zerah: So, he is a social worker as well as a baptizer?

Judas: He is not what we are looking for.

Simon: He is a powerful speaker. People hang on his every word even when he is condemning them. "You snakes, who told you that you could escape the punishment God is about to send? Do those things that will show that you have turned from your sins."

Zerah: That sounds like a Zealot.

Simon: He said more. "The ax is ready to cut down the trees at the roots. Every tree that does not bear good fruit will be cut down and thrown in the fire."

Zerah: Was he talking about the Romans?

Simon: No, he was talking about us, the chosen people of God.

Judas: *(sits)* Master, what Simon won't tell you is that soldiers come to John.

Zerah: And what does he tell them?

Judas: "Don't take money from anyone by force or accuse anyone falsely. Be content with your pay."

Zerah: Did he baptize them?

Judas: Yes. He welcomed them. He touched them, the unclean pagans.

Jude: Judas, don't be so dramatic. The Baptist wants all people to repent of their sins and turn to God. Maybe that is what God is saying to us through John.

Zerah: Jude, you cannot believe this. Telling Jews to repent is one thing, but to baptize our enemies is against everything I have taught you. Judas of Galilee gave his life fighting them. God will avenge his and other Zealot deaths one day.

Judas: *(stands)* We need a new King David. We need one who can convince all Jews to obey the law.

Simon: I think that is what John is trying to accomplish. He preaches sharing your food and goods with those in need. The Pharisees and the Sadducees do not preach this, yet they are considered the true interpreters of the law.

Jude: You mean the only interpreters of the law.

Zerah: Sons, God's Messiah will purge them, too. He will ...

Simon: *(interrupts)* use his ax to cut them down?

Judas: Yes, the Messiah will lead us to victory over our oppressors.

Zerah: He will purge the unlawful from our nation.

Jude: If that is so, then John is not the Messiah.

Judas: *(crosses upstage)* No, he is another misguided preacher.

Jude: He made me think.

Zerah: About what, Jude?

Jude: *(sits)* About the sins we all carry. About how we treat each other.

Zerah: But those who are zealous for the law and confess their sins do not speak to tax collectors and pagans.

Simon: *(sits)* Master, that's his way of bringing them to God.

Zerah: He is wrong. One must separate himself from anyone who does not only serve God.

Judas: Enough about John. Master Zerah, I believe the only way to deal with the Romans is to use the methods of the Sicarii and kill them whenever we have the opportunity.

Simon: The Sicarii are assassins and thieves — they are not Zealots. They violate the law by their actions.

Zerah: That is not entirely true. There are many descendants of Judas of Galilee who believe one serves only God.

Simon: But what about the murders they commit?

Zerah: That is where they are different from us. John is like them, though, in proclaiming the sharing of one's goods. I do have to admit that they do not practice this as they should. They have turned into an assassin group full of hatred for pagans and some Jews.

Judas: *(crosses downstage)* Can you think of a better way?

Zerah: I believe we must wait patiently for God to send deliverance.

Judas: I am tired of waiting. Our people are suffering and you all know it.

Jude: We do, but running around assassinating Romans will take years.

Simon: And cost many Jewish lives through Roman retaliation.

Jude: We should keep following our master's advice — pray and wait.

Judas: Doesn't God help those who help themselves?

Simon: *(stands)* Judas and Jude, do you remember what John said when people asked him if he was the Messiah?

Zerah: Do some think he is the *one* sent from God?

Simon: They had high hopes like us.

Zerah: What was his answer?

Simon: "I baptize you with water, but someone is coming who is much greater than I am. I am not good enough even to untie his sandals. He will baptize you with the Holy Spirit and fire. He has his winnowing shovel with him, to thresh out all the grain and gather the wheat in his barn; but he will burn the chaff in a fire that never goes out."

Jude: *(stands)* John speaks to you, Judas. Your King David is coming to purge us of Rome.

Zerah: John is a prophet. It will not be long. I feel it in my soul. Brothers, we must carry on our work of turning people back to God to get them ready.

Jude: We will, master.

Simon: Master, we are going to Galilee tomorrow. There is work there.

Judas: Maybe we should go to Jerusalem and find work. If the Messiah comes soon, surely he will appear there.

Zerah: Your namesake and my friend was from Galilee. Who knows where God's chosen one will appear? Thank you for your news. It is always good to see you. Perhaps we will be together in Jerusalem for the Passover.

Judas: And the arrival of God's Messiah.

Simon: Thank you, master, for your guidance.

Zerah: We have talked enough. Go and wash. Your room is ready. Supper will be ready soon. You can strengthen yourselves for your trip.

Jude: Master, we promise to pray and wait as you have taught. Right, Judas?

Judas: Yes, I will pray, but I cannot promise to wait.

Zerah: Judas, the Messiah is coming. Remember, God's time is not our time. Now go and get ready for supper. *(Simon, Judas, and Jude exit.)* Oh God, you know the suffering of your children. Please send your deliverer. We are ready to follow and restore your nation and bring glory to your name. You promised this land to Abraham. Fulfill your promise, I pray. May these eyes see the new King David and the new Israel.

(Lights go black.)

Scene Two

The home of Miriam and Abigail in Capernaum, a few weeks later

(Miriam enters as lights come up. She places a bowl of food on the table and arranges the furniture. Abigail enters with a bowl of fruit.)

Abigail: Here's the fruit, Miriam. It will be good to have Simon with us.

Miriam: I hope he arrives soon, I am getting hungry.

Abigail: *(puts bowl of fruit on table)* It has been a long time since we have had fruit like this.

Miriam: I've never seen our pomegranate tree do so well. *(turns to look at tree outside)*

Abigail: Didn't Simon's father plant that tree?

Miriam: Yes, Uncle Uri planted it for my husband, Nathan, because he made him a pair of Egyptian sandals.

Abigail: I miss Nathan and Uncle Uri.

Miriam: As I miss your husband, Elam. He was the best tanner in Galilee.

Abigail: You and Nathan were the only ones who would socialize with him.

Miriam: That was because of the smell of the tanner. It did take me a while to get used to it.

Abigail: He was such a good man that one easily forgot the smell of his work. *(looks off stage)* Where is our cousin, Simon?

Miriam: Your Elam was a Zealot like Simon. He taught Nathan and me so much about God's laws.

Abigail: He and Simon were close friends because of their zeal.

Miriam: They could argue all night over the smallest detail of the law.

Abigail: And your husband would have to quiet them down.

Miriam: Or, tell them a joke so they wouldn't be so serious.

Abigail: We had some wonderful times.

Miriam: I thank God for all we had with our husbands. They provided well for us. We have this house and garden, and even a few sheep.

Abigail: And we can afford to travel to see relatives and even go to Jerusalem once in a while for Passover.

Miriam: *(starts moving downstage)* But, without our mending work and Simon's help, we couldn't do all these things.

Abigail: I can't wait to tell Simon about our trip to Nazareth and all that is going on here in Capernaum.

Miriam: The new rabbi will impress him.

Abigail: I'm not so sure of that.

(Simon enters.)

Simon: So sure of what, Cousin Abigail?

Abigail: Simon, it is good to see you.

Miriam: Peace be with you, cousin.

Simon: Peace be with you. You both look well.

Abigail: Thank you. You must be tired from your trip. Sit and tell us about where you have been.

(Simon sits and Abigail and Miriam serve him and themselves.)

Simon: What were you talking about when I came in?

Miriam: *(sits)* Old times with Nathan and Elam and your father.

Abigail: *(sits)* Try one of these pomegranates from his tree.

Simon: Father was so proud of that tree. *(looks toward tree)* He used to tease Nathan, "You should have given me ten pairs of sandals for that fine tree." I miss him as much as I miss your husbands.

Miriam: Sometimes I wish that I could just talk to Nathan to tell him how much I love him.

Abigail: I feel the same about my Elam.

Simon: Right now I wish I could talk with my father about these crazy times we live in. I could use his advice.

Abigail: Doesn't Rabbi Zerah do that?

Simon: Yes, Judas, Jude, and I visited him on our way here. But my father always had the perspective of one not fully immersed in the law. He sent me to Zerah in order to learn the law.

Miriam: And now you can draw from both.

Simon: I try, but it isn't easy. So many Jews abandon the law and the Romans continue to make our lives harsh.

Abigail: We have a lot to tell you that may ease your mind, but tell us where you have been.

Simon: We built some barns for the wealthy Jews around Jericho. We also spent time listening to John the Baptist at the Jordan.

Abigail: Is he as powerful as we have heard?

Simon: He has a way of preaching that definitely gets your attention.

Miriam: We heard he has baptized many Jews.

Simon: True, but he baptizes Gentiles as well. Soldiers and other nonbelievers were washed by John.

Abigail: You don't seem impressed.

Simon: Many thought he might be the Messiah, but the "chosen one" would not touch Gentiles. We reported all we saw to Zerah and he feels the same.

Abigail: What was his advice to you, Jude, and Judas?

Simon: To pray and wait for God to send his Messiah. Jude and I agree with Zerah, but Judas is growing impatient. He thinks we should join the Sicarii.

Miriam: Don't they advocate violence against Romans and Jews who collaborate with them?

Simon: Yes, they are murderers and thieves. I'm not sure what Judas will do. We have work in Sepphoris. I am afraid Judas will join the Sicarii there. They have been active there.

Miriam: It is a Gentile town full of Romans. I don't like you going there.

Abigail: You don't seem to agree with Judas.

Simon: *(sits)* I don't know what to believe or do. Judas makes a strong argument. How long do we have to wait for God to deliver us? Maybe he wants us to take matters into our own hands.

Abigail: *(stands)* Simon, you have never been a violent man. You would not break the law.

Miriam: Your father would not approve of such actions.

Simon: I know. He was one who said a person draws strength from suffering as our people have done for centuries.

Abigail: Miriam and I have news that may help your spirit.

Simon: *(sits)* What news could you have that could ease my mind?

Miriam: We met a new rabbi from Nazareth who has a strong message and the power to heal and bring people to God.

Simon: What's his name?

Abigail: Jesus.

Simon: Jesus, the carpenter's son?

Abigail: Yes.

Simon: I have met him. He built some furniture for a house we built outside of Nazareth a few years ago. He has become a rabbi?

Miriam: We heard him speak at the synagogue in Nazareth. You won't believe what happened. He walked away from death that day.

Simon: What are you saying?

Abigail: We were in Nazareth to see Aunt Esther and went with her to the synagogue. In walked Jesus. He was taken to the front and handed the scroll of Isaiah. He unrolled it and read: "The Spirit of the Lord is upon me, because he has chosen me to bring good news to the poor. He sent me to proclaim liberty to the captives and recovery of sight to the blind, to set free the oppressed, and announce that the time has come when the Lord will save his people."

Miriam: Then he rolled up the scroll, sat down, and said, "This passage of scripture has come true today, as you heard it being read."

Simon: *(stands and crosses downstage)* That is outrageous. What did the men say?

Miriam: *(stands)* They were impressed. They said, "Isn't he the son of Joseph?"

Abigail: Then he insulted them.

Miriam: He said, "I am sure you will quote me the proverb 'Doctor, heal yourself.' I tell you this, a prophet is never welcomed in his hometown."

Abigail: Then he spoke of how Elijah and Elisha did miracles for people who were not Jewish instead of their own people.

Simon: What did that mean after quoting Isaiah's words?

Miriam: We're not sure, but it made all in the synagogue very angry. They dragged him out to the edge of town.

Abigail: *(stands)* Simon, they were going to throw him off the cliff.

Simon: Did they?

Miriam: We didn't get close enough to see what was going on, but suddenly we saw Jesus walk through the middle of the crowd and go on his way.

Simon: Common sense stopped them.

Abigail: I wouldn't say that. He seemed to have an unseen power that prevented them from carrying out their action.

Simon: *(turns away)* He is not a rabbi, but a magician.

Miriam: We have more to tell you. He came here to Capernaum and went to the synagogue and taught on the sabbath. We were all amazed at the way he taught because he spoke with authority.

Abigail: As he spoke, a man who had a demon in him, yelled, "What do you want with us, Jesus of Nazareth? Are you here to destroy us? I know who you are: You are God's holy messenger."

Miriam: Jesus looked at the man and said, "Be quiet and come out of the man." The demon threw the man down in front of us and went out of him without doing him any harm.

Simon: *(turns to them)* Jesus, the carpenter, can drive out evil spirits? Impossible!

Abigail: We were all amazed and said to one another, "What kind of words are these? With authority and power, this man gives orders to the evil spirits and they come out!"

Simon: *(steps toward them)* If I didn't know better, I would say you two have an evil spirit in you.

Miriam: He left the synagogue and went to Simon the fisherman's house. We heard he healed Simon's mother-in-law of a fever.

Abigail: That evening, people brought sick relatives and friends to the house. Jesus placed his hands on them and healed them all.

Miriam: Demons also went out of many people, screaming, "You are the Son of God."

Simon: That doesn't sound like exorcism. They still have the demon if they proclaim the carpenter to be the Son of God.

Abigail: We are not sure, but we did see crippled people walking away from the house.

Miriam: Simon, maybe Jesus is the one we have been waiting for.

Abigail: He has a way that we have never seen.

Simon: *(turns — then to himself)* Could Jesus be the one the Baptist said was coming?

Miriam: What did you say?

Simon: John the Baptist said one was coming who was greater than he is. I was wondering if he was talking about the carpenter. Has Jesus attracted many followers?

Abigail: Yes, Simon Peter and his brother, Andrew.

Miriam: And the sons of Zebedee.

Simon: Hardheaded Simon the fisherman follows Jesus? I don't believe you.

Abigail: It's true. Jesus was down at the lake teaching and when he finished he said to Simon, "Push the boat out further to the deep water, and you and your partners let down your nets for a catch." Simon looked shocked and told Jesus, "We worked hard all night long and caught nothing."

Miriam: Jesus just smiled at him, so Simon said, "But if you say so, I will let down the nets." They let down the nets and caught so many fish that the nets were about to break.

Abigail: They had to call for James and John to come and help them. They filled both boats so full of fish that they were about to sink. When they got to shore, Simon came to Jesus and fell on his knees and said, "Go away from me, Lord! I am a sinful man."

Miriam: Jesus laughed and said to all four of them, "Don't be afraid; from now on you will be catching people." They pulled the boats up on the shore, left everything, and followed Jesus.

Simon: *(turns away)* This is unbelievable.

Abigail: We said the same thing, but we saw it and are telling the truth.

Miriam: Simon, you must take Jude and Judas and go and hear Jesus. He probably will be at the synagogue on the sabbath.

Simon: I will. Zerah believes God's "deliverer" is coming soon. It is just hard to believe Jesus is the one.

Abigail: We plan to hear him speak whenever we can. Jesus has power to heal and drive out evil spirits. That power can only come from God.

Miriam: Perhaps he also has the power to deliver us from our oppression.

Simon: Judas and Jude are not going to believe this. I can hear Judas, "God's Messiah will never be a Galilean carpenter." *(laughs)* I can't wait to tell him all you have told me. They are staying with friends nearby. I must go at once and tell them about Jesus.

Abigail: If they don't believe you, bring them here and we will tell them.

Miriam: Simon, a new day is dawning in Israel. I really believe that.

Simon: I hope you're right. I will be back soon. *(exits)*

(Lights go black.)

Scene Three
The synagogue courtyard in Capernaum
(As lights come up, Jesus is on stage. Simon and Jude enter.)

Simon: Master, may we talk with you?

Jesus: Of course. What is on your mind?

Jude: *(sits)* We have many questions about your teachings. We have followed you for some time and still are confused by many of your words.

Jesus: Ask me whatever you wish.

Simon: *(sits)* We don't know where to start. But, we have been thinking about John the Baptist and his work. Teach us to pray just as John taught has disciples.

Jesus: When you pray, say this: "Father, may your holy name be honored; may your kingdom come. Give us day by day the food we need. Forgive us our sins, for we forgive everyone who does us wrong. And do not bring us to hard testing."

Jude: That's it?

Jesus: One does not need to say long prayers like the Pharisees do in order to draw attention.

Simon: God will hear and answer such a prayer?

Jesus: Suppose one of you should go to a friend's house at midnight and say to him, "Friend, let me borrow three loaves of bread. A friend of mine who is on a trip has just come to my house and I don't have any food for him!" And suppose your friend should answer from inside, "Don't bother me! The door is already locked and my children and I are in bed. I can't get up and give you anything." Well, what then?

Simon: You go back home and try to supply your friend's needs as best you can.

Jesus: I tell you that even if he will not get up and give you the bread because you are his friend, yet he will get up and give you everything you need because you are not ashamed to keep on asking. And so I say to you, "Ask and you will receive; seek, and you will find; knock, and the door will be opened to you."

Jude: Keep on asking and God will answer. We have done this, Master. But, God doesn't seem to answer us. We pray for deliverance from Rome and it doesn't come.

Jesus: Would any father give his son a snake when he asks for a fish? Or would he give him a scorpion when he asks for an egg? As bad as people are, they know how to give good things to their children. How much more, then, will the Father in heaven give the Holy Spirit to those who ask him!

Simon: So, we are not praying in the right way?

Jesus: Did you not hear the prayer I gave you? That is all you need.

Jude: I see. We will try harder to please God.

Jesus: You should always pray and never become discouraged.

Simon: That is not easy.

Jesus: That is because you do not always know what you are praying for. You place demands on the Father. That is not what I am teaching you.

Jude: Thank you, Master, but, we still are perplexed by your words and actions.

Simon: Why would you heal a Roman officer's servant? He is our enemy.

(Judas enters.)

Judas: Master, with all due respect, that was a violation of the law.

Jesus: How?

Judas: We are not to associate with Gentiles.

Jesus: Judas, you missed the point of what happened. The Centurion needed help, and God calls us to help anyone in need.

Judas: Even our enemies?

Jesus: Yes. Did you forget what he said? He didn't even want me to enter his home. He believed his servant would get well by my word. That is true faith. As I said, "Never have I seen such faith in Israel."

Judas: But, he is ...

Jesus: *(interrupts)* a creation of our Father just like us. Judas, you must see the bigger picture. God sent me to proclaim good news to all people starting with the children of Israel.

Simon: Master, our leaders would disagree. They say you violate the law when you heal on the sabbath and by associating with tax collectors and other outcasts.

Jesus: As I told the people, I did not come to abolish the law, but to fulfill it.

Judas: I don't see how you are doing that.

Jesus: All of scripture testifies to God's will and work in history, yet God's work is not complete. I do not say that the law is obsolete, but I confirm it. Remember that as long as heaven and earth last, not the least point or the smallest detail of the law will be done away with — not until the end of all things.

Jude: Is that why you go to those whom our leaders consider the wrong people?

Jesus: They have judged them as unworthy even though God created them just as he creates all people. Our leaders have not listened to the intent of the law, which is love of God and neighbor.

Simon: Is that why you taught us to not seek revenge when wronged?

Judas: *(moves toward Jesus)* Master, surely you didn't mean to teach us to turn the other cheek?

Jesus: The scriptures do not command revenge.

Judas: But, the law does tell us how to deal with crimes of murder, robbery, and other actions against one's neighbors.

Jesus: I am saying that there should not be unlimited revenge. One should not counter violence with more violence whether it is an individual, a community, or a nation.

Judas: How can you say this? No one can turn their cheek after being hit. The Romans have built an empire by not turning a cheek.

Jude: That doesn't make it right.

Simon: *(stands and crosses)* Master, I am still confused. You told us to turn a cheek, give up our shirt, carry a soldier's pack twice as far as he asks, and to lend anything our friends need. What does this mean?

Jesus: Others have selfish pursuits. You are not to act like them. You are to think of the needs of others before your own needs.

Judas: *(crosses away from Jesus)* That is crazy.

Jesus: No, that is love. You have been taught to reject those who do not belong to God's people and keep God's law, and you have done that. But, to do what God wants is to love impartially, just as he does.

Jude: *(stands and moves downstage)* If one practices this, they will be ridiculed.

Simon: *(sits)* Master, I hear you, but I agree with Jude. Do you want us to be expelled from Israel?

Judas: This way is not God's way.

Jesus: Whoever is near me is near fire; whoever is distant from me is distant from the kingdom.

Judas: *(sits by Jesus)* What does that mean?

Jesus: I have a baptism to receive, and I am distressed until it is over! Do you suppose that I came to bring peace? No, not peace, but division. From now on, a family of five will be divided, three against two and two against three.

Simon: So, to follow you will mean expulsion?

Jesus: Fathers will be against their sons, and sons against their fathers; mothers will be against their daughters and daughters against their mothers.

Jude: Master, you can't mean this.

Jesus: The road ahead is rough. If anyone wants to come with me, they must forget themselves, pick up their crosses, and follow me.

Judas: *(stands and moves away)* Rabbi, you are talking nonsense.

Simon: *(stands)* You are scaring me!

Jesus: *(stands)* Listen! We are going to Jerusalem where the Son of Man will be handed over to the chief priests and the teachers of the law. They will condemn him to death and then hand him over to the Gentiles, who will make fun of him, whip him, and crucify him; but three days later he will be raised to life. *(exits)*

Simon: What does he mean by those words?

Jude: We are going to Jerusalem where Jesus will fulfill his teachings.

Judas: *(moves to center)* He is talking like a madman. The Son of Man will not be killed, but will glorify God and reestablish his nation.

Simon: I don't think that is what our Master said.

Judas: He is not in his right mind. If Jesus is the Son of Man, I will make sure he fulfills his mission.

Jude: I am not sure you will change Jesus' mind, but I pray you can.

(Lights go black.)

Scene Four
At the cross

(Lights come up.)

Jesus: Father, forgive them for they don't know what they are doing.

(Abigail and Miriam enter.)

Abigail: How can Jesus say that after what they have done to him?

Miriam: I can't believe this is happening. He is such a wonderful teacher. He does not deserve crucifixion.

Abigail: *(moves toward cross)* Jesus, you healed so many; heal yourself.

Miriam: *(moves toward Abigail)* It is not going to happen. When the Romans nail one to the cross, they die.

Abigail: I curse these Romans and our leaders for doing this.

Miriam: I curse our cousin and the other disciples for not stopping this slaughter.

Abigail: Do you see Simon among this crowd?

Miriam: No, he is probably afraid to show his face.

Abigail: Or, he was arrested, too. He could be in jail right now.

Miriam: I don't think so. They wanted Jesus. Like the scripture says, "Capture the shepherd and the sheep will be scattered."

Abigail: I pray you are right.

Miriam: If anyone would fight for Jesus, it would be Judas. He always is close to being a killer like the Sicarii.

Abigail: *(moves away from cross area)* If that were true, he would be up there with Jesus. He talks tough, but I never saw him as one who would go around plunging a knife in any Roman he encounters.

Miriam: *(to Abigail)* You're right. That would violate his vow to obey the law.

Abigail: Miriam, let us leave this place. I cannot stand to see Jesus die.

Miriam: Oh, how I wish he could come down.

(As Miriam and Abigail start to move away, Simon appears.)

Simon: So do I.

Abigail: Simon, it is good to see you. I thought you might be in jail.

Simon: I wish I were.

Abigail: How can you say such a thing?

Simon: Look, Jesus is dying and I didn't do anything to stop it.

Miriam: I can't believe you just stood by and let them arrest Jesus.

Simon: *(turns away)* When it comes down to it, I'm a coward. I saw their swords and clubs and ran with the others.

Abigail: Where did they arrest Jesus?

Simon: *(turns toward them)* In the garden of Gethsemane — Jesus went there to pray after our Passover meal.

Miriam: How did they know you were there?

Simon: Judas led them to Jesus.

Miriam: Why?

Jesus: I thirst.

Simon: *(turns toward cross)* Oh, my Master, why did you allow this to happen? Why didn't you show your power to the council and Pilate?

Miriam: Simon, tell us about Judas.

Simon: *(turns toward them)* Like I said, we celebrated the Passover meal with Jesus. During the meal, he said that one of us would betray him.

Abigail: And that's what Judas did?

Simon: We all said to Jesus, "Surely you don't mean me?" Then I heard Peter and John whispering to Jesus. He dipped some bread in the sauce, gave it to Judas, and Judas left. We thought Jesus told him to go and buy what we needed for the festival or to give something to the poor.

(pause)

Miriam: Instead, he went and betrayed Jesus to the Romans. What a coward.

Simon: No, he went to the temple guards. They were the ones who arrested Jesus.

Abigail: Then how did the Romans get involved?

Simon: They took Jesus to the home of Caiaphas where the whole council met to try him. Peter and John followed to see what would happen. The council condemned Jesus and took him to Pilate.

Miriam: But, we heard that Pilate tried to release Jesus.

Simon: He invoked the custom of releasing a prisoner of the crowd's choosing in honor of Passover. He offered the crowd Jesus or Barabbas.

Abigail: Barabbas is part of the Sicarii. He has killed Jews as well as Romans.

Simon: Master Zerah called him an extremist. He said Barabbas forgot the spirit of the law in his anger against Rome.

Miriam: And the crowd called for him?

Simon: We tried to gain Jesus' release, but our leaders stirred up the crowd, convincing them to ask for the release of Barabbas.

Miriam: Was Judas one who stirred up the crowd?

Simon: I didn't see him. Pilate handed Jesus over to be executed. I don't think he wanted to, but the crowd was in such an uproar.

Abigail: How could they do this? Jesus did so much good and all of Jerusalem knows that. He healed at the temple and taught words of comfort to Israel.

Simon: He also chased away the animal sellers and moneychangers. He condemned our leaders for the way they teach and act. That is why they came for him. When he did these things, we thought he was getting ready to bring a revolt against Rome and usher in God's new kingdom. We thought he was the Messiah we have waited for and now he is dying.

Miriam: Didn't Judas feel the same as you?

Simon: I think that is why he betrayed Jesus. He thought that once Jesus stood before the council he would reveal himself as the Messiah even though Jesus never said he would.

Abigail: And when it didn't happen, Judas vanished.

Simon: Do not be so hard on Judas. Jude and I thought the same thing even though Jesus told us this would happen.

Miriam: What do you mean?

Simon: Before we came to Jerusalem, he told us that the Son of Man would be handed over to our leaders who would hand him over to the Gentiles to be crucified.

Abigail: You must not have heard him correctly.

Miriam: You mean Jesus is up there because it was meant to be?

Simon: It seems so. Cousins, you saw the power of Jesus. It seems that power is to be used for some purpose beyond our thinking.

Abigail: You are not thinking clearly. What you are saying is that Jesus wanted to die.

Simon: I don't know what to think. Jesus said many things we heard but wanted to ignore. He told us to turn the other cheek, love our enemies, and that he would be handed over to our enemies. We ignored the truth from God given to us by Jesus.

Miriam: Do you believe Jesus is God's Messiah?

Simon: I'm not sure, but I do know he is sent by God to teach us God's ways.

Miriam: But, torture and crucifixion cannot be the will of God for his messenger.

Abigail: God's servant, John the Baptist, also died a violent death, didn't he?

Miriam: Yes, but this can't be God's plan.

Abigail: Who can say they know the mind of God?

Jesus: My God, my God, why have you abandoned me?

Abigail: See, even Jesus does not know the mind of God.

Simon: *(toward cross)* Oh God, have mercy on us. Let your servant die. End his suffering. Bring him, all of us, peace. *(turns back)* Cousins, you should go home.

Miriam: And, where will you go?

Simon: I will stay until I understand why this happened.

Abigail: We will stay with you.

Simon: No, go; I will be all right.

Miriam: None of us will be right until we understand why Jesus is dying like this.

Simon: Master Zerah taught us that God's time is not our time. He is right.

Abigail: Have you seen him? He is here for the Passover.

Simon: No, I haven't even thought of him until today. I wish I could discuss all this with him.

Abigail: Maybe you will. We are going to our friend's home near the temple. You know where it is. Come and join us soon.

Miriam: *(toward cross)* Good-bye, Jesus. May God give you his peace.

Jesus: It is accomplished!

Miriam: He is dead.

Abigail: *(toward cross)* What does he mean?

Simon: He has completed the work God gave him.

Abigail: *(toward Simon)* So he is the Messiah?

Simon: Yes, Abigail, he is. Praise to God that we knew him.

Miriam: But, if he is the Messiah, why ...

Simon: *(interrupts)* Let it go for now.

Abigail: Simon, what is in your heart?

Simon: Jesus also told us the Son of Man would rise to life on the third day.

Miriam: *(turns toward Simon)* Impossible!

Abigail: Everything else Jesus said came true, why not that? Right, Simon?

Simon: We will see.

(Lights go black.)

Scene Five
Somewhere in Jerusalem, the next day
(As lights come up, Simon is sitting onstage and Zerah enters.)

Zerah: Peace be with you, Simon.

Simon: *(surprised)* Master Zerah, how did you know I was here?

Zerah: Jude told me. He sent me to bring you to the house all your friends are hiding in.

Simon: They are afraid of the Jewish authorities because we followed Jesus. I don't think we should act like cowards.

Zerah: Perhaps, but it may be the smart thing to do. You have lost your Jesus as I lost my Judas of Galilee. I wish you would have found me and introduced me to the carpenter. I heard so much about his words and actions.

Simon: Forgive us, Master, but with all that happened this week ...

Zerah: *(interrupts)* I understand.

Simon: Did Jude tell you about Judas?

Zerah: Yes. I can't believe Judas would cooperate with our leaders.

Simon: I can't believe he would betray Jesus for thirty pieces of silver!

Zerah: Judas always loved money a little too much.

Simon: Did Jude tell you what happened to Judas?

Zerah: Yes. He is devastated. He told me that the two of you found him hanging from an olive tree.

Simon: *(stands)* We buried Judas near here. Would you like me to take you there?

Zerah: I don't know if I want to pay my respects to someone who betrayed a fellow Jew and then killed himself.

Simon: But, he — all three of us — are like your sons.

Zerah: You and Jude did not violate the law like Judas did.

Simon: Jude and I believe Judas killed himself because he felt guilty.

Zerah: That may be, but it doesn't mean that we should forgive him. He condemned himself by his actions.

Simon: Master, Jesus predicted Judas' betrayal. He told us that one of us was going to betray him. Maybe Judas could not help doing what he did.

Zerah: Yes, he could. Judas did not have to make the prediction come true.

Simon: *(turns away)* After following Jesus, I'm not so sure.

Zerah: Tell me about the carpenter. From what I have heard, he was not a true Zealot, but a misguided preacher and healer who gave our people false hope.

Simon: That's not true. He was a great teacher. He gave our people comfort and hope. He erased their minds about our plight as God's chosen people. I could tell you many things, but I'm not sure where to start. *(sits)* He confused us to the very end. That is why I am sitting here, trying to figure out what his work means.

Zerah: Talk to me, Simon. Maybe I can help you.

Simon: Many times I wanted to come to Jericho to talk to you about what Jesus said and did, but we were so caught up in following him that we didn't want to leave him.

Zerah: I can see he has influenced you and Jude in a way that no other has.

Simon: Master, I truly believe Jesus was sent to us by God.

Zerah: If that is so, why is he dead?

Simon: That is what I have been asking myself.

Zerah: And, have you figured it out?

Simon: I'm not sure, but I will try to explain it to you. Jesus did not practice the Zealot way. At first, this bothered me, but he had such a way about him that I could not leave him.

Zerah: When I heard you three were following him, I wanted to come and knock some sense into you. Is it true Jesus ate with outcasts?

Simon: Yes, he said, "Those who are healthy do not need a doctor, but only those who are sick." Jesus not only healed people from diseases and drove out evil spirits; he healed the souls of many who you say are unworthy.

Zerah: I heard he even healed a Roman officer's servant.

Simon: He did. He told us he had never seen such faith in Israel as the faith of that Centurion. He healed that servant without even seeing him.

Zerah: No one could do that.

Simon: Unless he was sent by God. Master, Jesus was different from other rabbis like your Judas of Galilee. He taught us something new. It took us a long time to see that, so how can I convince you?

Zerah: *(turns)* You can't. Jesus was wrong. God would not send one who violates the law of Moses.

Simon: Jesus came to fulfill the law. He taught us that the most important commandments are to love God and our neighbor as we love ourselves.

Zerah: But, the Romans are not our neighbors.

Simon: That is what we have always believed. Jesus brought a new way of looking at all people. He taught us to see all as God's children.

Zerah: Is it true that a tax collector was part of your group?

Simon: Yes. Matthew was called by Jesus. None of us accepted him at first, but Jesus taught us to accept him because we all are sinful as he was.

Zerah: You have abandoned all that I taught you.

Simon: *(stands)* No, what you taught us was only partial. Jesus brought us the true message of God. He taught us love.

Zerah: I can't believe I am hearing this. You are rejecting all we Zealots believe. Love belongs to only those who obey the law.

Simon: You are wrong.

Zerah: How dare you challenge me! Jews cannot love those who tax them; those who force them to live under such harsh conditions. Tax collectors and Romans are unworthy. They do not deserve our respect, let alone our love.

Simon: Master ...

Zerah: *(interrupts)* Stop calling me that. You insult me by insisting that what I have taught you is wrong. I came here to learn about this carpenter and what I have learned is that he taught a false doctrine.

Simon: Jesus did not teach a false doctrine. He taught the true word of God. Jude, Judas, and I were as confused as you, but now I see things more clearly.

Zerah: If Jesus was so right, why is he dead?

Simon: *(turns)* I cannot answer that. All I know is that I am beginning to understand his way through his death.

Zerah: That makes no sense.

Simon: Jesus said we are to love our enemies and pray for those who persecute us.

Zerah: He was crazy.

Simon: He showed us that as he died. As they lifted him up, he cried, "Father, forgive them because they don't know what they are doing."

Zerah: He was out of his mind because of the pain inflicted on him.

Simon: I don't think so.

Zerah: Simon, how can I get you to come to your senses? Jesus is not worthy of your devotion. He broke the law. That is why they killed him.

Simon: Zerah, you teach building up the body. Jesus taught building up the spirit.

Zerah: What does that mean?

Simon: You believe the way to save Israel is to build up a body of believers who will be true to the law and to God. Jesus taught that one must build up their spirit before they can build up the body.

Zerah: Many prophets have said this and they were killed, too.

Simon: That is because we don't want to love. If the Romans were chased away, another group would replace them.

Zerah: How do you know that?

Simon: Look at the history of Israel. We have been conquered by many nations.

Zerah: And, we have rid ourselves of them.

Simon: You know that isn't entirely true. Jesus taught us that all people are worthy to God whether they are Jews or not. If you believe God created all things, then all people are his.

Zerah: But, he chose us to be his people. That will never change.

Simon: No, it will not; but Jesus taught us that all people need God. Our job is to teach that to others, even our enemies. If we don't, people will continue to fight each other.

Zerah: *(turns away)* I will not believe this.

Simon: I now see that this is why Jesus died; so we could be forgiven and then pursue his message of love.

Zerah: I will never love a Roman or a tax collector.

Simon: Jesus sacrificed his life so that we might turn our lives around. He said, "The greatest love a person can have for his friends is to give his life for them."

Zerah: *(turns back)* Do you believe Jesus is God's Messiah?

Simon: I do.

Zerah: You are out of your mind. He died like a common criminal. If he were the Messiah, he would have raised an army.

Simon: I believe that is what Judas hoped when he betrayed Jesus. He thought Jesus would stand before the council and rally them around him to overthrow the Romans. But that was not his mission. His mission was to bring God's love to all people, and he had to die to accomplish this.

Zerah: I have heard enough. Simon, you are not the person I knew. This Jesus has put you under some sort of spell. I will pray for you to come to your senses.

Simon: You will believe when Jesus comes back to life.

Zerah: What?

Simon: Jesus told us all that would happen to him here in Jerusalem. We didn't want to believe him, especially Judas, but it all came true. He also told us that three days after his death, he would rise to life.

Zerah: Simon, you have an evil spirit in you. This is impossible. No one can return from the dead.

Simon: God's Son can.

Zerah: I am sorry for you. You are so wrong. Jesus was not God's Son.

Simon: I used to believe that, but now I know. Jesus had the power to do whatever he wished and he chose to use his power to demonstrate God's love for all people — Jews and Gentiles. And, he will rise to life to seal the truth of his message.

Zerah: Simon, I no longer know who you are. I never want to see you again. You have sinned against God and me. *(exits)*

Simon: Master Zerah, I will pray for you to see the truth of Jesus.

(Zerah exits — pause.)

Simon: Oh God, I pray for all to see Jesus' message. All are worthy to you. May all people see that and love each other as you love us.

(Lights go black.)

Easter Vigil

Introduction

Day Of Nothing – So Why Are We Here?

A Worship Service with a choice of two Meditations
by Mary Hoover and Amy Jo Jones

Will You Live In The Light?

A Worship Service and Meditation
by Mary Hoover and Amy Jo Jones

The Living Will And Testament Of Jesus Christ

A Worship Service and Meditation
by Mary Hoover and Amy Jo Jones

Easter Vigil
Introduction

Three Saturday Night Vigil Services

Holy Saturday can be a day of nothingness, and even a day where one might feel lonely and lost. For others, Holy Saturday is just another ordinary day. Last-minute preparations are being made for Easter. Easter clothes are being pressed and cleaned, and the church is usually decorated with lilies, hyacinths, and tulips on Saturday. Good Friday is over, Easter is next.

But what about Holy Saturday? Holy Saturday can be a day of emptiness and sadness for some. It can feel like the day after a funeral or a traumatic, life-changing event. Anyone who has experienced the death of a loved one can sometimes feel the same emotions of loss after they have heard the passion story read on Good Friday. Have you ever imagined what your life would be like without Jesus? What would you feel? What were the disciples feeling the day after? The answers are endless.

Sometimes, a day of emptiness and nothingness can also serve as a day of renewal as well as reminding ourselves that we are called to live in the light of Christ in times of peril, war, prejudice, and global upheaval. Participants are invited to renew their baptism. These worship services can be used for renewal purposes.

These services are being presented as they were when given to Trinity Church, United Methodist in Yorkville, Illinois. Each person is invited to adapt these services for the specific needs of their particular congregation. Each worship service is different from the other.

In the worship service, "A Day Of Nothing — So Why Are We Here?" the Call To Worship is written by Mary Hoover. In the second and third worship services, all Prayers are adapted from the *United Methodist Book of Worship*. The suggested hymns are from the *United Methodist Hymnal*.

The Meditations, "A Day Of Nothing — So Why Are We Here?" "Will You Live In The Light?" and "The Living Will And Testament Of Jesus Christ" are written by Mary Hoover.

The choric, "Lost Without Jesus," is written by Amy Jo Jones. This choric can be used in place of the Meditation, "A Day Of Nothing — So Why Are We Here?" if you want to involve more than one person for the meditation. A choric is a reading that is read by many voices, sometimes separately, sometimes in unison. Readers reading in unison are emphasizing a particular point by joining voices and reading as one voice. In order to understand a choric before it is performed, each reader must understand the choric as being a monologue, that is, a single voice where all voices are to be as one voice, speaking at different times and expressing different emotions. The selected readers are invited to be stationed in various places in the sanctuary, depending upon the design of the sanctuary. Or, all of the readers can be standing together in the front or back of the sanctuary. Microphones are suggested for each reader.

Suggested prelude and postlude songs for "Lost Without Jesus" are Michael Card's "Why?" for the prelude and "You Are The Light Of The World" for the postlude. Twila Paris' "Hold On" is also a suggested postlude song.

We pray that you are blessed by these services and that your journey with Christ is deepened by them.

— Amy Jo Jones and Mary Hoover

Easter Vigil
Worship Service

Day Of Nothing — So Why Are We Here?

Opening Music

Welcome And Announcements

Call To Worship
Leader: Why are we here on this Holy Saturday? Why have we come on this day of nothingness?
People: **We have come because we are lost without Jesus. We want to have hope.**
Leader: Why are we here on this Holy Saturday? Why have we come when it appears there is nothing we can do?
People: **We have come because we are lost without Jesus. We don't know what else to do.**
Leader: Why are we here on this Holy Saturday? Why have we come on this day of nothing but pain and sorrow?
People: **We have come because we are lost without Jesus. We long to move out of our grief and to love again.**
Leader: Why are we here on this Holy Saturday? Why have we come?
People: **We have come because we are lost without Jesus. We long to know and share his love.**
All: **But why are we here? We are here because we have journeyed through Holy Week with Jesus. We are here to find him in our lives and once again give our lives to him.**

Opening Hymn   "Be Still, My Soul"

Prayer Time

The Lord's Prayer

Hymn Of Preparation   "Are Ye Able?"

Scripture Text   Matthew 27:57-66

Meditation   "A Day Of Nothing — So Why Are We Here?"
or "Lost Without Jesus" (choric)

Offering

Closing Hymn   "Lord, I Want To Be A Christian"

Sending Forth And Blessing
    May you go and turn your moments of "nothingness" into sacred time with God. May you be filled with and know the peace and love of Jesus Christ now and forever. Amen.

Easter Vigil
Meditation

A Day Of Nothingness — So Why Are We Here?

There are few of us who haven't had to face the day after the funeral, the day after the burial of someone we love. Sometimes the "day after" is a day of nothingness.

Some feel like they are caught in a time warp. The world, the people, and life moves all around us, but we seem to be stuck. During the time of preparation for the funeral, there had been so much activity, so many things to do, so many people to see and to contact. We can be saturated. And then it comes — everything is over. We had to leave the grave. We had to leave the cemetery. We had to get beyond the tomb. The "day after" can be a day of nothingness. It can be that day where we say, "Stop the world, I want to get off."

For the disciples and the followers of Jesus, the day after his death and burial was also a day of nothingness. Some of the disciples and followers tried to stay out of sight and did nothing to call attention to themselves. They were fearful of being known as having any connection to Jesus. Some of them gathered in small groups to pray and comfort each other. Others may have returned home. They probably felt a wide range of emotions: fear, doubt, confusion, guilt, sorrow, pain, loss, emptiness ... the list is endless.

The gospels don't say much about the day after the death and burial of Jesus. The gospels seem to skip to Easter morning. Only Matthew has a few verses, and it has been suggested that these verses are not historical, but arose at a time where there were charges that the resurrection was a hoax and the disciples had stolen the body of Jesus. The verses from Matthew were introduced to show that not even an official act of Pilate could prevent the resurrection. Even these verses appear to be as nothing. Let's hear these verses together.

> *When it was evening, there came a rich man from Arimathea, named Joseph, who was also a disciple of Jesus. He went to Pilate and asked for the body of Jesus; then Pilate ordered it to be given to him. So Joseph took the body and wrapped it in a clean linen cloth and laid it in his own new tomb, which he had hewn in the rock. He then rolled a great stone to the door of the tomb and went away. Mary Magdalene and the other Mary were there, sitting opposite the tomb.*
>
> *The next day, that is, after the Day of Preparation, the chief priests and Pharisees gathered before Pilate and said, "Sir, we remember what that imposter said while he was still alive, 'After three days I will rise again.' Therefore command the tomb to be made secure until the third day; otherwise his disciples may go and steal him away, and tell the people, 'He has been raised from the dead,' and the last deception would be worse than the first." Pilate said to them, "You have a guard of soldiers; go, make it as secure as you can." So they went with the guard and made the tomb secure by sealing the stone.*

There might be some real scriptural value in these verses. There is something in them that gives "nothingness" some importance and worth.

First of all, it is indicated that the day after Jesus' burial was the day after the preparation day. That makes it the sabbath — a day of rest — a day of worship, prayer, meditation, and reflection — but a day of rest. It is time to be spent in the presence of God — a time for you, me, and God to spend together. Sabbath is a time for us to listen to God, to be taught, to be comforted, to be nurtured and restored. What happens to be "nothingness" can actually be a time of transformation: of allowing God to touch and love us. When we allow God to come that close to us, we can do "nothing" but empty ourselves of ourselves and be filled with love — God's love for us and our love for God. That is when "nothingness" becomes sabbath. That is when it becomes holy. That is when "nothingness" becomes "sacred time."

For us to be what God wants us to be — whole, healthy, and productive people — that is, disciples of Christ, we need sabbath time. We need holy and sacred time with God. Too often we see that time as a time of doing nothing. We see it as nonproductive. In today's world, being nonproductive is not seen as a good thing. Because of that attitude, we often shortchange and even rob God of time. It is time that could be spent with God, so that God can touch our lives and make us whole and even make us more productive people. So, what keeps us from sacred time with God?

Perhaps it is exactly what Matthew tells us: The rock was rolled in front of the tomb and then sealed and guarded. That is what keeps us from sacred time with God. This is not to suggest that Jesus was stolen or that the resurrection is a hoax. Jesus is alive. Instead, what is suggested is that we are the ones who seal ourselves off from God and guard against entering into sacred time with God. Maybe it is because we stay hidden behind those rocks of fear, pain, sorrow, doubt, guilt, loss, and emptiness ... all those emotions we mentioned before and then some. Perhaps it is because we hide behind rocks of sin, such as stubbornness, selfishness, greed, pride, and prejudice. In our woundedness, we wonder, "What can God do?" We ask ourselves, "What can God do for us?"

Here is what God can do. Centuries ago, the day after Jesus' burial, the day we perceive as "nothing" happening, was a day of sabbath for Jesus and God. They had sacred time together, time spent transforming Jesus to his eternal glory — to life everlasting. And then the rock was rolled away so that Jesus Christ might reach out to everyone and offer us life everlasting.

Whatever our rock is on this Holy Saturday, allow Jesus to reach out and roll it away so that we might enter into sabbath time with God. Let us use the rest of this day to enter into holy and sacred time with God. Tomorrow, let us come to celebrate the transforming power he has in our lives.

Let us pray: Gracious and loving God, we give you thanks and praise for the importance of "nothingness" in our lives. We ask that you help us to see those times as productive times to be spent with you, allowing you to enter our lives so that we might be transformed by your power. Help us to utilize these moments of "nothingness" and live them as holy and sacred moments. In the name of your precious Son, Jesus Christ. Amen.

Easter Vigil
Meditation

Lost Without Jesus

This is a choric for seven people. A choric is a reading for several voices. When the print is in bold, directed voices are to read in unison. The mood of this choric is pensive, angry, and sad, ending in sadness and on the edge of hopelessness. It's the voices of several people grieving the crucifixion of Jesus. The scattered voices should represent the human mind and spirit being shattered in their thoughts and hearts because of the grief they might be feeling. For effect, the group should stand in front of a plain, white sheet or a rock.

Voice 1: It's like a fog.
Voice 2: I can't believe what I saw yesterday.
Voice 3: Was it yesterday?
Voice 4: I lose track of time.
Voice 1: My mind is in a blur.
I can't think.
I can't sleep.
I can't remember when I ate last.
Voice 5: All I remember is what I saw.

Voice 1: I am in shock.
Voice 5: I am dismayed.
Voice 3: My heart feels like it is exploding.
Was it yesterday?
Did all of this happen yesterday?

Voice 1: All I remember is what I saw.
Voice 6: The bloody cross.
The dangling corpses
hanging like slabs of meat.
Vultures flying overhead
waiting to prey on the dead.
The ground covered with blood.
The place of the skull covered with human bones.
The gray skies.
The darkness.
Voice 1: The darkness.
Voice 2: The darkness.
Voice 4: Yes, the darkness.

Voice 1: No light.
Voice 3: The veil of the temple being torn.
Voice 1: The earthquake.

Voice 4:	Jesus just hanging there. His body dripping in blood.
Voice 2:	I watched. I watched the Breath of Life fling itself into the heavens for the last time.
Voice 5:	Watching them take him off the cross. Watching the rolling stone and hearing the loud thud.
Voice 6:	The loud thud crushed my heart.
Voice 2:	Did this really happen? Was it yesterday?
Voice 1:	This is a bad nightmare. Jesus, you can't be dead.
Voice 3:	I'm horrified!
Voice 4:	His death is an outrage!
Voice 2:	I want to scream!
Voice 4:	My heart feels like one huge blowtorch of flames burning within me.
Voice 1:	Sadness. Anger. Outrage. Anguish.
Voice 4:	It's beyond words.
Voice 5:	I can't believe he's gone.
Voice 1:	I can't believe I heard him say,
Voice 7:	"It is accomplished."
Voice 3:	What is accomplished?
Voice 2:	What is accomplished by his death?
Voice 3:	Now he's gone.
Voice 1:	Dead.
Voice 2:	He's in the tomb.
Voice 5:	Sealed.
Voice 1:	The stone is so heavy no one can move it.
Voice 6:	It's final.
Voice 2:	Why the guards? What's the point?

Voice 1:	All of this smells of politics ... making it seem that someone is in control.
Voice 3:	Killing someone to make it seem like the world will become a better place.
Voice 5:	Killing someone in order to keep a sick political system intact.
Voice 2:	It's all about keeping people in the dark.
Voice 1:	Can't we learn?
Voice 6:	How can our world become a better place with such reprehensible and despicable behavior?
Voice 4:	How can one human being do that to another?
Voice 6:	How can we be so cruel as to kill the innocent?
Voice 3:	What was it that he did that was so terrible for him to be killed like a common criminal?
Voices 1-6:	**Everything is out of control.** **Everything is out of control.**
Voice 1:	The whole world has gone mad to have killed a man like Jesus. He said,
Voice 7:	"It is accomplished."
Voice 2:	What is accomplished in his death? Is this real? Did this happen?
Voice 1:	My hope has been shattered. It's been uprooted like a tree blown over by a storm.
Voice 7:	At least there's hope for a tree as long as it is rooted. Even if it is cut down, it will renew itself. Even if its roots are old in the earth. At the scene of water it will bud and produce branches like a sapling.
Voice 1:	But Jesus is gone. He's dead.

Voice 7:	All humans languish and die.
	If a man dies, can he live again?
Voice 5:	My hope is gone.
Voice 4:	What happened to him who said,
Voice 7:	"I am the light of the world."
Voice 4:	What happened to him who said,
Voice 7:	"I am the Good Shepherd."
Voice 4:	What happened to him who said,
Voice 7:	"I am the bread of life."
	"I am the living water."
Voice 3:	Were his words empty?
Voices 1-6:	**What's the point of his death?**
	What do these things mean?
Voice 1:	It seems like the enemies have triumphed.
	Everything is going to go back like it was.
Voice 5:	I don't want that.
Voice 1:	I was finding hope in his words.
Voice 3:	In his life.
Voice 4:	In his love.
Voice 1:	Now everything is gone.
Voices 1-6:	**My life is ruined.**
Voice 1:	I can't live without him.
	I'm in the dark.
Voice 2:	I feel like a sheep wandering in the desert.
Voice 1:	I'm starving for any kind of nourishment.
Voice 7:	My soul thirsts for the living God.
Voice 1:	The living God.
	That's who I thought he was ...
Voice 6:	And he's dead.
Voice 4:	Gone.
Voice 7:	O God, where are you?
	It seems like if I look to the east, you are not there.
	If I look west, I can't perceive you.
	If I look north, you are concealed.
	If I look south, you have hidden yourself.
Voice 4:	Where are you?

Voice 1:	Don't you leave me, too!
Voice 6:	God, I'm lost without him.
Voices 1-7:	**I'm lost without Jesus.**

Voice 3: Why have you forsaken me?
Why have you forsaken the whole world?
Why have you taken the only hope I ever had
away from me?

Voice 1: I can't live.
Voices 1-7: **I can't live without Jesus.**

Voice 4: He who said,
Voice 7: "I have come so that you might have life
and have it to the fullest."
Voice 5: Where is he?
Where is his life?
Voice 1: I'm empty.
Voice 2: I just want to scream into the heavens!

Voice 3: Where is that spirit he promised who would
be with me, who would come again
to counsel me and teach me all things?
Voice 1: I need him.
Voice 6: He's gone.
Voice 1: My life has been destroyed along with his.
Voice 4: I want to die.
Voice 1: I want to curl up and fade away.
There's no point in living if he is not alive.

Voice 3: I loved him so much.

Voice 1: Now I have no place to go with that love ...
The love he gave to me.
The love I gave to him.
Voice 4: His love for me made me feel like I could do anything.

Voice 2: In fact, he said,
Voice 7: "You are my friend if you do what I command you."
Voice 1: And all he commanded was to love.

Voice 3: A strange command.
Voice 4: Because one cannot be commanded to love.
Voice 1: The compelling factor about that command
is that I wanted to keep it.
Voice 2: I wanted to love.
Voice 5: I wanted to love as he had loved me.

Voice 1:	I wanted to give to the world as he had given to me. I wanted others to find life as I had found life in him.
Voice 2:	Maybe that's all that command means. Maybe all that command means is that I can be like him and be full of his life if I love. Because I love. I don't know anything else. I don't know how to do anything else.
Voices 1-6:	**But he's gone.**
Voice 6:	He's dead.
Voice 2:	Where is my hope?
Voice 1:	My whole life is nothing without him.
Voices 1-7:	**I can't live without Jesus.** **He is the center of my life.**
Voice 3:	Did it take his death for me to realize this?
Voice 1:	Did it take this for me to realize that I have no center without him?
Voice 4:	How can I go on? What can I do?
Voice 2:	What is the point of being in this world without him?
Voice 7:	Have mercy on me, O Lord, for I languish; heal me, O Lord, for my bones shake with terror. My whole being is stricken with terror, while you, O Lord — how long? O Lord, turn! Rescue me! Deliver me as befits your faithfulness. For there is no praise of you among the dead; in Sheol, who can acclaim you? I am weary with groaning; I melt my couch in tears. My eyes are wasted by vexation, worn out because of all my foes. Away from me, all you evildoers, for the Lord heeds the sound of my weeping. The Lord heeds my plea, the Lord accepts my prayer.

All my enemies will be frustrated and stricken with terror;
they will turn back in an instant, frustrated.

Voice 1: God, I wish that I could see the frustration of my enemies.
Of Jesus' enemies.

Voice 2: When are they going to be stricken with the same
kind of terror that I feel?
When am I going to feel like you hear my prayer?
Do you even hear the sound of my weeping?
Can you hear my cry?

Voices 1-7: **I am lost without Jesus.**
Voice 6: I can't live without him.
Voice 2: He is the center of all that I am.

Voice 1: He is the reason why I live and breathe.
Voice 5: He is the reason why I see.
Voice 1: He is the reason why I love.
Voice 2: He is the reason why I can love.

Voices 1-6: **Can I ever love again without him?**

Voice 1: My heart is so shattered
so torn
so smashed and crushed.

Voice 7: The eyes of the Lord are on the righteous.
His ears attentive to their cry.
The face of the Lord is set against evildoers,
to erase their names from the earth.
They cry out and the Lord hears,
and saves them from all their troubles.
The Lord is close to the brokenhearted;
those crushed in spirit, he delivers.
Though the misfortunes of the righteous be many,
the Lord will save him from them all,
keeping all his bones intact,
not one of them being broken.
One misfortune is the deathblow of the wicked,
the foes of the righteous shall be ruined.
The Lord redeems the life of his servants;
all who take refuge in him shall not be ruined.

Voice 1: Come to me, Lord. I am brokenhearted.
Voice 6: I am crushed.
Voice 1: Hear my cries.

Voice 2:   I can't be alone in this.
Voices 1-7: **I can't live without Jesus.**
Voice 1:   I can't live at all.
             Life has no purpose without Jesus in my life.
Voice 3:   Is there any hope?
             Isn't there a glimmer of hope?
             Anywhere?

(A candle is lit behind the sheet or stone; a spotlight growing brighter will serve just as well.)

Voice 2:   Where is the light of the world?
             Where is the light shining in the darkness?
             Is there any hope?

(Silence for a period of time ... as the candle grows brighter ... perhaps more than one candle or a spotlight that is on a fade switch may work.)

Easter Vigil
Worship Service

Will You Live In The Light?

Opening Music

Welcome And Announcements

Call To Worship
Leader: My brothers and sisters in Christ:
People: **On this most holy night we, like the disciples, gather together to pray and grieve in the darkness of our world. We grieve for the darkness in our world. For we, like the disciples, feel as if the darkness has overcome us. But there is hope, for Jesus said, "I am the light of the world. Whoever follows me will never walk in darkness, but will have the light of life."** (John 8:12)

Opening Hymn   "Christ, Whose Glory Fills The Sky"

Prayer *(in unison)*   Psalm 22:1-5
My God, my God, why have you forsaken me? Why are you so far from helping me, for the worlds of my groaning? O my God, I cry by day, but you do not answer; and by night, but find no rest. Yet you, the praise of Israel, are enthroned in holiness. In you our forebears trusted; they trusted you and you delivered them. To you they cried, and were saved; in you they trusted, and were not put in shame. In you we still trust; save us from our darkness, we pray. Amen.

Hymn Of Preparation   "I Want To Walk As A Child Of The Light"

Meditation   "Will You Live In The Light?"

Offering

Prayer Of Dedication *(in unison)*
Gracious God, giver of light, we ask that you accept our tithes and gifts. Use them to dispel the darkness in the world. Use them, O Lord, to bring others the radiance of Christ's love. In his name we pray. Amen.

Closing Hymn   "This Little Light Of Mine"

Sending Forth And Blessing

Easter Vigil
Meditation

Will You Live In The Light?

For three voices

(Lights are on in the worship area. An unseen voice begins to speak.)

Voice 1: My God, my God, why have you forsaken me? *(pauses)*
Father, forgive them for they do not know what they are doing. *(pauses)*
I am thirsty. *(pauses)*
It is finished. *(pauses)*

(Immediately the lights are turned off in the worship area.)

Voice 2: In the tomb of darkness our hearts cry to you, God, "My God, my God, why have you forsaken us?" Why have you returned us to darkness? Perhaps it is that we never left the tomb of darkness. Could that be it?

Voice 1: I am the light of the world. Whoever follows me will never walk in darkness, but will have the light of life.

Voice 3: We live in the darkness of conflict.
Conflict in families.
Conflict between races.
Conflict between nations.
We live in the darkness of conflict.

Voice 1: I am the light of the world. Whoever follows me will never walk in darkness, but will have the light of life.

Voice 3: We live in the darkness of greed.
People are starving.
People are homeless.
People are cold and in pain.
And yet, we do not share. We live in darkness.

Voice 1: I am the light of the world. Whoever follows me will never walk in darkness, but will have the light of life.

Voice 2: We live in the darkness of violence. We abuse our children. We abuse women, men, and minorities, and even the elderly. We abuse each other when we do not get our way. We are a people living in the darkness of violence.

Voice 1: I am the light of the world. Whoever follows me will never walk in darkness, but will have the light of life.

Voice 2: We live in the darkness of prejudice. We hold judgments and suspicions against men, women, African Americans, Latinos, Jews, Muslins, and even other Christians. We hold attitudes and judgments against gays, lesbians, those with AIDS, and those with disabilities. We live in the darkness of judgment and suspicion toward others.

Voice 1: I am the light of the world. Whoever follows me will never walk in darkness, but will have the light of life.

(As this is being said, the Christ candle is carried forward and placed on the altar.)

Voice 2: Look at the light of Christ. We know the Easter story. We know we can live in the light of the resurrected Christ! So why? Why do we live in the tomb of darkness? Are we afraid if we live in the light, we will see more clearly? Are we afraid when we see more clearly, we will have to do something to dispel the darkness? If we stay in the darkness, death wins. Christ is calling us.

Voice 1: Come follow me. I am the light of the world. Whoever follows me will never walk in darkness, but will have the light of life.

Voice 3: So let us follow Christ. Turn on your light, leave the tomb, dispel the darkness, and become one in Christ, bringing light and hope to the world. Let us pray: God of life, through Jesus Christ you have bestowed upon the world the light of life. Sanctify this new fire, and grant that our hearts and minds may also be kindled with holy desire to shine forth with the brightness of Christ's rising that we may attain to the feast of everlasting light; through Jesus Christ our Lord. Amen.

Easter Vigil
Worship Service

The Living Will And Testament Of Jesus Christ

Prelude

Welcome
    Welcome to our Easter Vigil Service. We hope this service might help to prepare us for the celebration of Christ's resurrection tomorrow morning and that it might give us a deeper sense and understanding of who Jesus is and what he is giving us. Let's begin our service of worship.

Call To Worship
Leader: Dying, Christ destroyed our death.
People: **Rising, Christ restored our life.**
Leader: Christ will come again in glory.
People: **As in baptism WE put on Christ;**
              so in Christ may WE be clothed with glory.
Leader: Do you not know that all of us who have been baptized into Christ Jesus were baptized into his death? Therefore, we have been buried with him by baptism in death, so that, just as Christ was raised from the dead by the glory of the Father, so we, too, might walk in newness of life. For if we have been united with him in a death like his, we will certainly be united with him in a resurrection like his.

Opening Hymn   "When I Survey The Wondrous Cross"

Prayer Of Confession And Pardon
    Holy God, before you our hearts are open, and from you no secrets are hidden. We bring to you now our shame and sorrow for our sins. We have forgotten that our life is from you. We have neither sought nor done your will. We have not been truthful in our hearts, in our speech, in our lives. We have not loved as we ought to love. Help us and heal us, raising us from our sins into a better life, that we may end our days in peace, trusting in your kindness unto the end; through Jesus Christ our Lord, who lives and reigns with you in unity of the Holy Spirit, one God, now and forever. Amen.

Leader: In Christ you are forgiven. For who shall separate us from the love of Christ? Shall tribulation or distress or persecution or famine or nakedness or peril or sword?
People: **No. In all things we are more than conquerors through the one who loved us. We are sure that neither death nor life, nor angels, nor principalities, nor things present, nor things to come, nor powers, nor height, nor depth, nor anything else in all creation, will be able to separate us from the love of God in Jesus Christ our Lord. Thanks be to God. Amen.**

Hymn Of Preparation   "To God Be The Glory"

Scripture Reading   Romans 6:6-11

Meditation "The Living Will And Testament Of Jesus Christ"

Offering

Prayer
Leader: Gracious and loving God, as we have inherited your kingdom, and as we have received this inheritance, we ask that you use and multiply these gifts so that through them, others might believe and receive. In Jesus' name. Amen.

Closing Hymn "The Day Of Resurrection"

Sending Forth And Blessing
 When you exit, you will find the baptismal font placed at the rear entrance of the church. As you walk past, touch the water and then touch your forehead and renew your baptismal vows. Remember that you are baptized, and be thankful.

Leader: And may the God of all grace, who has called us to eternal glory in Christ, establish and strengthen you by the power of the Holy Spirit, that you may live in grace and peace. Amen.

Postlude

Easter Vigil
Meditation

The Living Will And Testament Of Jesus Christ

This is the Living Will and Testament of Jesus Christ.

I, Jesus Christ, the Son of God, Creator of heaven and earth, Lord and Savior for all; being grace, mercy, and love, do declare this to be my living and continuous will.

To everyone — to everyone who believes in me, I, freely and without condition, give eternal life.

To those who have come, to those who will come, and to each of you, being my brothers and sisters, being children of God, I leave all that I possess and all that I am; for I give to you the kingdom of God. The kingdom of God is within you. You can truly live in the image of my Father in heaven. It is living in God's image that you will establish my kingdom here and now. I leave this to you.

You are heirs of the kingdom. You inherit the kingdom now. For in your baptism through the Holy Spirit, we are united, and in being united, you have died with me and are resurrected with me. You do not have to wait for eternal life. You do not have to wait for the kingdom of God. I give them to you now. You belong to eternity now, even though it feels as if you are stranded in time. You are citizens of the kingdom of God now. Live your life as resurrected Easter people. Live as kingdom people, for you know me and therefore know the kingdom of God and how to live. Live now. Don't wait. Eternal life is not later, it's now.

As resurrected people, as kingdom people, I give you forgiveness for your sins. I give you forgiveness so my forgiveness can flow through you to others. Receive my forgiveness. Give my forgiveness. Give that now. Don't wait. Don't hang on to hurts and sadness. Forgive.

I give to each of you my joy — my peace — and my love. I leave these things to you so that you may be free, free from worldly bondage, in order to live. To live generously — to live abundantly. I have come that you might have life, and have it to the full. Live as I have commanded you. That is to *love* — to love God and to love one another as I have loved you. Even now — even now I love you. Love now. Live now.

I leave with you the power of the Holy Spirit. In that power we will always be joined and be of one mind. You will always have that connection to me because I am the vine and you are the branches. Let my love and life flow through you so that you will be like a tree planted by waters, revealing your fruit in due season. Be rooted and grounded in me. Whenever you feel afraid, confused, or lost, you will remember that I am with you, that we are one, and your well-being will return to you because of your connection to me. With the Spirit, you will receive guidance, discernment, and wisdom. Constantly, through prayer, seek these things so your life will become as my life, which continues on forever.

This is God's will and mine, that you become like me, that we become one and of one heart. In doing that you reveal the kingdom of God.

Become the answer to the prayer that I taught you. In that prayer, you praise and honor our Father by saying, "Our Father, who art in heaven, hallowed be thy name." In praying these words you recognize the supremeness of God, to be God of all, and yet you understand your smallness in his power and majesty. You recognize the mystery of the great "I AM." God is everywhere and you cannot be anywhere in the universe where God is not present. Live in that awe.

Recall the words you pray next. "Thy kingdom come, thy will be done, on earth as it is in heaven."

Hear what you are asking: God's kingdom to come, and God's will to be done, here — here on earth just like it is in heaven. Bring heaven and earth together. Unite it as one. Be a mirror of what goes on in heaven. Be a mirror and image of me. Live as you have been created to live. Unite us as one with God, and one with each other so you, too, may be made perfect like me. This is what you are asking for.

I tell you that in my death and resurrection, I have left you the keys to obtain the answer to that prayer. The answer is you. You are the key. You are the answer. I remind you that through your baptism you have died with me, you have been buried with me, and you have been resurrected with me. You are a new creation for this world — for this life. And later, when you physically die, you will be transformed again into a new realm becoming even more perfect in God's love. When I, Jesus Christ, come again, you will be there, also.

I do not want you to worry about your future. Do not ask, "Will I go to heaven?" or "Will God receive me?" Instead, I want you to live now the eternal life I have given you. You are in heaven now. You are living in eternity right now. My suffering, death, and resurrection become meaningless if you will not receive this inheritance from me.

Live in the kingdom of God!
Live eternally!
Live richly and abundantly!
Live generously with joy and peace!
Live a life of love!
Live now!

This is the inheritance I leave to you. This is my living will left to everyone. Believe and receive. Become a channel of my peace, love, and joy.

Now let us join together in the prayer I taught you to pray.

Our Father, who art in heaven,
    hallowed be thy name.
    Thy kingdom come,
    thy will be done on earth as it is in heaven.
Give us this day our daily bread.
And forgive us our trespasses,
    as we forgive those who trespass against us.
And lead us not into temptation,
    but deliver us from evil.
For thine is the kingdom, and the power, and the glory,
    forever. Amen.

Easter Day

Do You Believe?*

A Monologue
by Amy Jo Jones

Mary Clopas

A Monologue
by Diana M. Morris

*This is part three of a three-part monologue series using the same character.

Easter Day
Monologue

Do You Believe?

Character
This is intended for the pastor to deliver to the congregation.

Music Suggestions For Easter Sunday
"Love Crucified, Arose" by Michael Card
"Crown Him" by Michael Card
"At The Font We Start Our Journey"
"Christ Has Risen"
"Christ The Lord Has Risen Today"
"Easter People, Raise Your Voices"
"Thine Is The Glory"
"He Lives"
"I Come To The Garden"

Pastor: I want to finish telling you a story that happened to my family and me during a Passover in Jerusalem 2,000 years ago. I told you a couple of days ago that I saw how Jesus died ... Jesus, my best friend in the world ... Jesus, the only person in the world who made me feel important. I watched him die. It still remains the worst thing I have ever seen in my life, and I was only ten years old when I saw it.

After Jesus had been taken down from the cross, Daddy picked me up and carried me in his arms to where we were staying. Nothing made sense. I had lost my lamb. I had lost my best friend. I was terrified. It was the only Passover ever that we did not celebrate. It wasn't intentional, we just forgot to do it. We were so sad and scared. Besides, what was there to celebrate?

I cried myself to sleep the night that Jesus died. My parents couldn't explain this death to me any more than they could explain to me why the Passover lambs had to be sacrificed in such a brutal and horrible way, and then we would eat them to celebrate the Passover. They couldn't explain to me why something had to die in order for us to remember how God loves and cares for us all the time. Was there any real reason to any violence? All of these things were whirling through my mind as I fell asleep ... I was exhausted.

When I woke up, I discovered that I had slept for three days. It was really early in the morning when I woke up. I went outside and wandered around the empty streets of Jerusalem. Everything seemed like a ghost town. I started thinking about my lamb that I had lost ... I hoped that at least he was safe. My heart was still shattered, and I wondered if I was ever going to feel any better. I missed my woolly friend. It was hard to remember what day it was, and if my life had any purpose.

As I wandered the streets, I started kicking a rock and followed it to wherever I kicked it. I did not pay attention to where I was going. I just followed the rock. Kicking that rock eventually led me to Golgotha, that hill where they executed people and let their bodies stay out there for the vultures. My rock landed in a pile of broken bones. I looked up, and realized where I was. I saw the empty cross. I relived the whole event of watching Jesus die again and started screaming at God as to why he would take my best friend away. I was just as terrified as I was three days ago. I did not like Golgotha.

I left Golgotha, forgetting the rock I was kicking, and I went to a small garden area. I paid attention to where I was going this time. I had heard that Jesus had prayed there and spent time with his other adult friends who followed him. I stayed there. I sat under a tree, with my head tucked between my knees and was hugging my knees against my chest. I started to cry. My sides and lungs ached so much from sobbing that I just sat there and rested and cried. I was so lonely. I really missed Jesus. Would I ever have anyone like him in my life again?

As I sat there, with my head tucked between my knees, I felt someone touch me. It scared me and I jumped, but I stayed all huddled. Maybe if I didn't look up, the person would leave, I wanted to be left alone. The stranger was so patient, though. He must have known that I was terribly thirsty, because he gave me some cool water to drink. Crying makes you thirsty, if you didn't know that. He seemed to understand that I was scared and upset about something. He saw my tear-stained face. He started to stroke my hair and he wiped away my tears from my closed eyes. He didn't seem to care that I did not want to open my eyes. Nothing was said between us for a while, and I never opened my eyes while he was caring for me. Something about this man felt familiar, but I was not sure. There was only one other grown up who had treated me like I mattered, and he was dead. I wondered who this person might be.

He finally broke the silence and asked me a question. In his voice, I heard a lot of love — like what I was going to say really mattered to him. He asked me, "Why are you out here all by yourself?" And then everything tumbled out of me. I told him how scared I was at that awful bloody mess I had seen three days ago, and how my best friend was murdered right in front of me. I told him that I had lost my lamb, that I was terrified and miserable, and that my parents couldn't explain this to me. I told him how confused I was. It was like a dam had burst, I had so much inside of me that I needed to say to anyone who would listen.

Something seemed familiar about this man. I had been so full of tears and spilling my heart to him, that it did not occur to me that I should ask this person who he was. He was listening with such concentration. I finally asked him who he was. He said, "Don't you recognize me?" Until that moment, I hadn't even opened my eyes to even see what he looked like. I looked up and looked straight into the eyes of Jesus ... and I screamed! It was Jesus! I couldn't believe it ... but I had to believe it! I jumped up and climbed the tree that I was sitting up against. I hugged that tree with all my might. This couldn't be true!

I gasped and said, "Jesus, you're supposed to be dead ... are you a ghost?"

Jesus chuckled and said, "No, I'm not a ghost, and I am not dead anymore. I've risen from the grave."

"What? How?" I started pummeling him with a hundred questions, most of which started with "How?" Jesus threw back his head and laughed at me and looked at me with gleaming eyes. He was so delighted to see me asking all these questions. He told me to get out of the tree so he could talk to me. I climbed down, but kept my distance. I was not sure if he was a ghost or what ... this was too spooky!

He said to me, "Do you remember when you tried to save me, when you called my name, and your daddy grabbed you before you could touch me? Do you remember when I was carrying the cross and suffering, that I looked at you? Do you remember that I looked at you?"

I said that I did.

He said, "What did you see in my eyes? Think now. Think past the tears and the fright you were in, and remember what you saw."

Then I remembered. I said, "I remember. You told me with your eyes that you were going to be okay. Is this what you meant?"

He threw back his head and laughed out loud again. "Yes, this is exactly what I meant! I couldn't tell you then that I was going to rise again after three days, and that I had to die in order for this to happen. But I wanted you to know that I would be okay, and you would be okay, too. You need to stop crying now, because I am alive! You have to remember, since God is a part of all this, he and I together had the biggest laugh. I never intended to stay dead, because my Father in heaven did not intend for me to stay dead. Those soldiers and leaders of the church did not have the last word. Violence never has the last word — love does. My Father did ... and I think it's a good one, don't you?"

Then he explained to me that this had to happen in order to be able to obey his Father in heaven completely. He must have seen the confused look on my face, because he explained to me how he was God's Son and that God had sent him here to this earth to show everybody how to treat one another. Violence does not have the last word — love does. He told me that is why he loved me so much, because God loved me. God showed him how to love me. He kept going on and explaining this to me, and I'll never forget one of the things he said to me. He said, "Because I have loved you and will always love you, you are to do the same thing that I do and copy me, even down to what I think and do ... you will be able to do this because I will always be with you and show you how. If you pray, keep focused on me, and listen to me all the time, you will become just like me; you can even do greater things than I can."

My eyes started to light up. This was really the coolest thing in the world. It all made sense now! Of course, he had to be God's Son! This explained everything — why Jesus treated everybody like they were somebody, and loved them all. He was God in the flesh. Wow — I could even think what Jesus thought and do as he did, and pray as he prayed. I started to realize that I could be Jesus with skin on, and I wanted that more than anything.

I started thinking up hundreds of questions. I could see that it was Jesus in his eyes. I never forget someone I have looked in the eyes. But yet, I needed to be really sure. I knew Jesus was real, because he had touched me, but I wanted to be really sure. I frowned, thinking hard.

He asked, "What's wrong?"

I said, "I need to know that it is you for sure. I need to be really sure."

Again, he threw back his head and laughed. His laughter filled the trees. He seemed to understand everything that I was thinking and understood that this was all so new and wild to me, that it had to be some kind of dream. He was so patient with me. I knew he wanted me to understand.

He said, "I want to show you something." He showed me his wrists, where they had driven the spikes. I looked, and there were scars where the holes in his hands and wrists had been. He offered to let me touch his hands, and I touched them. I knew then that it was really Jesus. But Jesus wanted to make sure that I really knew, and he showed me his feet. The scars were huge! I touched every inch of them.

Then, Jesus told me to look at his head, around his eyes and his scalp. I saw the scars from the huge gouges the thorns had made in his head. I touched those, too, and felt them. I was so glad that Jesus let me touch him in this way, so I could remember how it felt.

Jesus went one step further and showed me his back and his side. I touched the scars all down his back from those whips that took his skin away. His whole back was scarred, and if I hadn't known what had happened, I would have thought Jesus had been in a fire and his skin had been burned off. However, even though it was so scarred, his back was completely healed.

I was spellbound by this experience. Jesus was letting me touch all of his scars. He was letting me see and be sure that it was him. I still didn't understand how he could come back from the dead, healed, but scarred. Maybe the scars are always there to remind us of the pain of the past, but they don't have the last word. Violence does not have the last word — love does.

While I was touching Jesus, to make sure it really was him, he kept talking to me. He told me that I was one of the first people that he had shown himself to, and that people, in general, were not going to believe this. It was strange; it had never happened before. People were going to be frightened with this kind of information and not believe it at first. They may even think that I was crazy — and that's okay, because I've always been a little crazy, so I had to be clever in how I revealed this good news in order that people would believe it, but not to worry if others didn't get it right away. What mattered was that I lived what I knew to be true. He told me that it would be by the way I lived my life that people would come to believe. Actions speak louder than words.

He told me how to convince people that he was truly risen. He said, "You have just had some terrible things happen in your life. You slept for three days because you were so miserable that I had died. Well, I'm not dead anymore. You can't act like I'm dead anymore. You can't leave me in the tomb because I'm not there. I don't want you to forget the awful things you saw, but you need to remember that whatever awful things happen in your life, they do not have to keep you from living. My scars need to remind you that even though I have healed completely from this, my scars remain so you or I won't forget the pain of this world.

"You can't stop awful things from happening anymore than you could have stopped me from dying. But, you can remember that scar tissue is more important to have as a sign of who I am rather than leaving me among the walking wounded and dead. The message I want you to give to the church is that they are my body and blood. Tell them to live like it and be me with skin on to those whom they meet. Their skin will show the same scars as I have because there will be those in this world who will still try to kill me again and again. Just remember that it's more important to show off my scars and know that I am alive, rather than to leave me among the wounded and dead. Be my body and blood to the world.

"You've seen me. You know that I have defeated death. You have touched me. I have touched you. You have listened to me. I have listened to you. We have looked each other in the eyes. You know that I am alive. You have to live like you've seen me and believe that I will live forever. I want you to be happy, full of love, and full of me. I have the final word. I have won, and so will you. My love will be made complete in you if you embrace my life completely. Do you believe this?" With that question, he then told me he needed to go and talk to his disciples. And he vanished.

I was left to wonder about all these things. Everything was starting to make sense now. He had the final word, not the bad stuff that happens in this world. Violence does not have the last word — love does. He wants us to live what we believe and be winners. He doesn't want us to lay down and play dead when bad things happen to us. We aren't supposed to cry defeat in our lives if we know that Jesus is alive. I think that is what resurrection really means. We may have the scars of our past hurts, but Jesus is the one who heals us and gives us new life and a reason to live and be happy people, full of him.

I started home. I was whistling and smiling. None of this made any sense, but I knew that it was true, because I had touched and talked to Jesus. As I walked, I heard a baa-ing sound in the thicket. There was my lost lamb! I caught him up in my arms and held him close to me. I was delighted and so happy. Jesus was alive. I had found my lamb. Things could not be any better in this world. I went home to tell my parents what I had seen. I knew that they would believe me ... and they did. Do you believe this story?

*This is part three of a three-part monologue series using the same character.

Easter Day
Monologue

Mary Clopas

Character
> Mary Clopas

Props
> None required

Setting
> None required

Costume
> Use period costume

Mary Clopas: *(quietly and yet questioning)* He is risen — my Lord — my nephew, Jesus. There is new life for all of us. *(looks at congregation)* You probably don't know much about me. My name is Mary and I am married to Clopas. We, too, live in Nazareth, near our families. My sister is also named Mary, which was confusing many times. She is my younger sister and the mother of Jesus. I have watched Jesus grow from a toddler to his ministries at age thirty and to his death. But now I know he was *not* just the boy and the man I knew, but he *is* my Lord, the Messiah, and he's *alive*!

How can this be? He certainly did die on Friday. I know because we three were there at the foot of the cross; that is, his mother, Mary; Mary Magdalene; and myself. We saw him die and we stood there when the Centurion put that sword in Jesus' side. We had heard all his words before, especially to his mother and to his disciple, John, who was with us. She is under John's care now.

My sister followed Jesus in so much of his ministry. She was in the background and yet he knew she was there. I couldn't understand on Friday why he had to be killed, but Mary understood. I don't know how she handled being there, seeing Jesus in such pain and agony, hearing his breathing get more shallow, and knowing he was being tortured right there in front of her eyes. I was so worried about her, my sister. Mary is such a lovely person. She has a deep soul and is such a great listener. In recent months, she has finally told me of the angel, Gabriel, and her pregnancy with Jesus. At first I thought she had lost her mind. But I have come to believe that everything she has told me has been true.

I had given birth two months before Mary, so when she, Joseph, and Jesus came back from Egypt, our sons were very close and they loved to play together.

I can't believe it. He is risen!

There was that time not long ago when Jesus' friend, Lazarus, died, and days later, Jesus came to their house and he raised Lazarus from death and he told us to unbind him, to help Lazarus be free again.

Jesus didn't have to die, you know. He had the same free will as the rest of us. He could have decided to live and have a normal life, have a family, and continue as a carpenter. He was a good one, like his father, Joseph. God didn't *make* him die. Jesus chose to die in our place, each one of us. I can hardly keep my wits about me when I think of this, when I wonder at the love he has for each of us. When I think of that beating and those nail holes, I just cannot keep from crying, even on this wonderful resurrection morning.

He is risen! Say it with me: He is risen! He is risen! Again, so loudly that you really believe it: He is risen! Hallelujah!

About The Authors

Joe Barone has ministered to various congregations for several years, including First Christian Church (Disciples of Christ) in Carrollton, Missouri, and First Christian Church (Disciples of Christ) in Windsor, Missouri. He is a graduate of the University of Missouri and holds a Master of Divinity degree from Phillips Graduate Seminary in Enid, Oklahoma. He is the author of *About A Loving God* (CSS).

Joseph M. Beer is the pastor of Mt. Laurel United Church of Christ in Gray, Pennsylvania. He has written, directed, and performed in religious and historical dramas for the past 25 years. He has a Doctor of Ministry in religious drama from Lancaster Theological Seminary.

William R. Grimbol is a Lutheran pastor living in Sag Harbor, New York. In addition to parish ministry work, he is involved in the larger community and continues an avocation of creative writing.

Mary Hoover is a member of Trinity Church, United Methodist, in Yorkville, Illinois. She is a certified Lay Speaker, as well as a preschool teacher. She lives with her husband, Harold, and together they have two children and one granddaughter.

Amy Jo Jones is an ordained elder in the United Methodist church in Northern Illinois Conference. She graduated from Garrett Theological Seminary in 1994. She is a graduate in sacred music and organ from the University of Notre Dame. She has served in several parishes in the Chicago area. Currently, she is a hospice chaplain residing in Beaverton, Oregon.

Jeff Milsten is the pastor of Trinity Lutheran Church in Longview, Wisconsin. He attended the University of Virginia and then later, Gettysburg Seminary. Prior to serving in Longview, he served other Lutheran churches in North Carolina and Idaho. He lives with his wife, Shannon, and their three children.

Diana M. Morris has served in various pastoral roles in the United Methodist and Disciples of Christ churches over the past twenty years. Most recently, she is serving as the writing minister at Gender Road Christian Church (Disciples of Christ) in Canal Winchester, Ohio, along with various Ohio women's ministries. She earned degrees from Capital University (Columbus, Ohio) and Methodist Theological School in Ohio (Delaware, Ohio).